Real-World Project Management

New Approaches for Adapting to Change and Uncertainty

Mary Feeherry DeWeaver, Ed.D.
and Lori Ciprian Gillespie

QUALITY RESOURCES.
A Division of The Kraus Organization Limited
New York, New York

Most Quality Resources books are available at quantity discounts when purchased in bulk. For more information contact:
Special Sales Department
Quality Resources
A Division of The Kraus Organization Limited
902 Broadway
New York, New York 10010
800-247-8519

Printed in the United States of America

01 00 99 98 97   10 9 8 7 6 5 4 3 2 1

Quality Resources
A Division of The Kraus Organization Limited
902 Broadway
New York, New York 10010
212-979-8600
800-247-8519

The paper used in this publication meets the minimum requirements of American National Standard for Information Sciences—Permanence of Paper for Printed Library Materials, ANSI Z39.48-1984.

ISBN 0-527-76321-7

Library of Congress Cataloging-in-Publication Data

DeWeaver, Mary Feeherry.
    Real-world project management: new approaches for adapting to change and uncertainty / Mary Feeherry DeWeaver, Lori Ciprian Gillespie.
        p.   cm.
    Includes bibliographical references and index.
    ISBN 0-527-76321-7 (alk. paper)
    1. Industrial project management. I. Gillespie, Lori Ciprian, 1956-. II. Title.
    HD69.P75D49   1997   96-53330
    658.4'04—dc21   CIP

Contents

The Project Management Challenge: Dealing with Uncertainty

The premise of this book is that risk and uncertainty are inherent in project management but that the project manager who accepts this fact can identify the uncertainties that are likely to occur and mitigate the risks they present. In this book we document the most important lessons we and our colleagues have learned about dealing with uncertainty and risk from our collective experience in managing a variety of projects for the past three decades.

Like most project managers we know, we enjoy the challenge of managing projects, but we also admit that the constantly changing work environment and the increasing demands of the competitive economy have created ever-greater levels of frustration and uncertainty for project managers and their teams—despite advances in technology that have provided tools that should make it easier to manage projects and carry out project work. Our attempts to deal with this frustration and uncertainty led to the writing of this book.

Our objectives are to help project managers:

- Apply the lessons learned through experience by successful project managers.
- Take a proactive approach to dealing with rapid and unpredictable change.

- Anticipate and deal with uncertainty by using change management strategies and tools.
- Develop a new approach to your project management roles.

About This Book

The information in this book reflects our own experience, of course, but also the comments, problems, insights, and solutions collected during interviews and focus groups, in person and on-line, with project managers and experts who work in many diverse fields and in a variety of specialties. We asked these colleagues to describe problems they have encountered at different stages of project management and in their different project roles and to identify what types of problems were most critical. We also asked them to share their good experiences in managing projects and the lessons they have learned from these experiences.

Organization

The book is organized into nine chapters that can be read in the order presented, or in any order that meets your current need. A list of additional resources and references is found at the back of the book, because no one book can provide in-depth coverage of the many topics that relate to project management. The bibliography lists the books and articles we found most helpful in the writing of this book.

In chapter 1, we discuss the characteristics of projects and the reasons for the increasing popularity of conducting business through projects. We describe our overall attitude toward project management, and we discuss the different contexts in which we anticipate that project managers reading this book may be working; for example:

- Newly independent entrepreneur.

- Intrapreneur.
- New technical professional.
- Leader of a self-managed team.
- Experienced project manager.

In chapter 2, we describe the linear approach to project management and give some examples that illustrate the use of this approach. We then make the case for a less linear, more holistic process. In chapter 3 we discuss this recommended project management process and explain why it is better able to accommodate uncertainty and change and mitigate the risk they pose to projects.

In chapters 4 through 6 we explore in detail how the application of this approach mitigates risks project managers are likely to encounter in these three important roles:

- Politician.
- Human resources manager.
- Change agent.

In chapter 7 we discuss risks commonly encountered at the different stages of a project and suggest strategies that can be used to decrease these risks.

Finally, in chapter 8, we offer general recommendations and list errors that project managers must avoid if they are to be successful in this age of uncertainty and change.

Chapter 1

Project Management Today

Project Management as a Process or as a Way of Life

Managing a project can be a challenging and satisfying experience. But it can be a frustrating and destructive one if you're unprepared for the uncertainty and unanticipated change that are inevitable over the life of most projects today.

Uncertainty Is Inevitable

Uncertainty is the natural state of the universe, and the ability to cope successfully with it is the key to survival for every species. Although uncertainty will always be present in every aspect of project management, you can avoid its worst effects—and even turn some to your advantage—by being prepared to anticipate it and developing strategies to cope with it.

Because uncertainty is inevitable, we believe that project managers must view uncertainty and unanticipated change as simply normal project events that can be dealt with and planned for, using the strategies and tools that successful managers have developed.

The Concept of a Project

What is a project? *Webster's* calls it a plan or scheme, an undertaking requiring a concerted effort, arranged by mutual agreement and accomplished together. On the basis of this definition, you and everyone you know has, at one time or another, managed a project. Have you ever planned a wedding, a class reunion, or a Girl Scout cookie sale or organized a golf outing, a soccer tournament, or a major home remodeling? All of these undertakings involved a plan that had to be accomplished with the help of other people. You were a project manager without even knowing it! You also probably had some experience in dealing with uncertainty—for example, rain canceling an outdoor event or illness of a player jeopardizing the team performance.

In the work environment, a project is expected to produce specific products or services. The project manager is responsible for planning the project and for ensuring that project activities will lead to accomplishing the project goals, which usually include making a profit—in spite of uncertainties and difficulties.

A few types of work have always been done in a project context. For example, when civil engineers bid on a project to construct a water system, they study the terrain, determine what resources are required to do the work and what staff capabilities are needed, and then submit a proposal to the municipality, explaining how they would carry out the work. Competing proposals are submitted by all the engineering firms that want to bid on the job. The funding agency reviews the proposals, selects one (usually after extensive negotiation), and awards the contract to build the facility to the firm with the winning proposal. The project ends when the system is completed, and the project team disbands.

Projects versus Traditional Work Organizations

Until relatively recently, however, this kind of project work was common only in certain fields or organizations. Most work, instead, was accomplished by permanent staff, organized in departments, in fixed hierarchies that could be diagrammed on an organization chart. Employees were hired to perform work as part of on an ongoing process, according to their job descriptions.

Most work was performed in a production environment and was continuous, from day to day. Resources were provided depending on the volume of work. Supplies were stored at a central point and provided on request. The work people did day by day was relatively routine. Risk was low and predictable, and there were many levels of supervision and management.

Projects, by contrast, are organized as needed, to produce specific one-time results. Instead of a continuous flow of predictable work, project teams perform unique tasks, with labor and other resources assigned to the project based on task requirements and charged to the individual project budget. Risk and unanticipated change, which are of minimal concern in traditional production environments, are endemic to project environments. Project tasks are more complex, and people on projects must take more responsibility for their own work, because there is less management oversight than was common in production environments. Unlike traditional continuous work processes, project work has a definite beginning and end. A successful project must be completed on time, within budget, and according to agreed-upon specifications. Risk and change can affect a project manager's ability to satisfy any or all of these success measures.

The Increasing Popularity of Projects

Organizations today have adopted a project approach to many types of work for a variety of reasons, including:

- Major changes in the economy that have changed the way consumers use products and services.
- Increased competition and the resulting need to respond to challenges from new competitors with new services and products.
- New and increasing numbers of customer requirements, resulting in a need to develop new ideas and bring new products and services to market more quickly.
- Extensive downsizing to decrease costs that puts additional pressure on the surviving staff to be more productive.
- The ability of information technologies to integrate work processes, breaking down traditional departments and eliminating the need for many types of jobs.

Because of these pressures, many business, nonprofit, and government organizations have found it useful to abandon their pyramidal bureaucracies, because hierarchical organizations and staffs with fixed jobs and unspecified goals and tasks are less able to respond quickly and creatively to these new realities. Using a project approach allows organizations to quickly focus on priority needs, flexibly assign staff, apply new technology in creative ways, and deliver products and results more quickly than they could have using their traditional organizational structure.

Fortune magazine's issue on "The End of the Job" pointed out that, "As a way of organizing work, the traditional job is becoming a social artifact, created in the 19th century and well suited to the demands of a newly industrial world, but poorly adapted to a fast managing, information-based economy." "The demise [of the job] confronts everyone with unfamiliar risks. . . . Today's organization is rapidly being transformed from a structure . . . of jobs into a field of work needing to be done" (Bridges 1994, 62–74).

New, flatter organizations using a project approach can hire or assign workers on an as-needed basis to accomplish specific tasks and get new products and services to market more cost-effectively and faster than the competition. A project team can be organized to do a job more rapidly than any one traditional department within an organization because the skills required are likely to be in different departments that were not designed to work together. Projects work toward measurable goals, and progress toward these goals can be continually tracked. Individuals can be assigned to projects, and their time charged directly to specific project tasks. As tasks are completed, these individuals can be replaced by others, who have the expertise for the next tasks. A project can be staffed with exactly the talent it requires, by using internal staff or a mix of internal staff and temporary workers; and a project team can be quickly disbanded when its work is completed.

Because it is so flexible, the project approach is increasingly employed in disciplines as diverse as software development, manufacturing, human resources, and even retail sales. The project managers we interviewed for this book illustrate the wide range of areas in which a project approach is used to accomplish work.

What Does This Mean to You?

The growing popularity of working through projects means that your success, and the success of your organization, may depend upon your developing or improving your ability to manage projects effectively and profitably. At its most productive, working through a project structure can:

• Lower overhead cost because time and resources can be billed against specific tasks and because the project manager takes on the responsibility for many overhead functions.

- Increase the likelihood of more immediate return on investment because costs are closely tracked and monitored, and payment is received based on task completion over the life of the project.
- Establish accountability for work accomplishment.
- Make more productive use of staff because people can be assigned to defined tasks and reassigned to other projects when their tasks are completed.

However, you will gain these results only if you understand how to maximize the advantages of the project approach to work and resist the urge to reinstate more traditional ways of doing business. If your project management style replaces the old bureaucratic management structure with an equally rigid project management process and structure, you will not enjoy the flexibility and advantage that a project approach offers.

Problems with Current Project Management Approaches

Managing projects has become increasingly difficult for several reasons. As a project manager, you are expected to see that your team produces high-quality work, produces it quickly, and produces it at a price that is lower than your competitors. To be really successful, you must also satisfy the customers so well that they will want a long-term relationship that will generate repeat business. In addition, if you are a project manager within a publicly traded company, your project may be expected to generate a rapid return on investment that will enhance the value of the organization's stock.

This is a tall order, and many current projects are failing to achieve one or more of these expected outcomes. Project managers cite several reasons for this:

- Projects are too complex.
- The pressure to achieve results more quickly impacts quality.
- The short half-life of technologies results in rapid obsolescence of project processes and products.
- People and organizations resist the changes that projects are intended to achieve.
- Project managers and teams lack the tools and know-how to deal with uncertainty.

This last point is the focus of this book. Although every project has unique features, nearly all projects include common aspects that spell the difference between success and failure. We believe that the most important of these is the project manager's ability to deal proactively with uncertainty and change and with the risks they present to the successful completion of the project.

Do You Need Project Manager Skills?

A project manager must be able to: plan the project, set goals, identify specific tasks to be accomplished, specify the skill sets needed to accomplish the project tasks, staff the appropriately skilled project team, and direct and empower all team members to use their skills to advance the project goals.

If you don't need these project management skills now, you most likely will as projects become the preferred way to do business throughout the economy. Further, if you are now, or expect to be, in one of the roles described in the next paragraphs, you will certainly need project management skills.

Are You a Newly Independent Entrepreneur?

Project managers may be newly independent entrepreneurs who offer their services to a variety of clients. Often, these entrepreneurs have left corporations, either involuntarily because of downsizing or voluntarily often because of a lack of opportunity for advancement in existing flattened organizations. We can expect that the number of entrepreneurs will increase. Movement from the predictable world of the organization into the uncertain, highly challenging world of the independent entrepreneur is growing.

Business Week (Mandel 1994, 90) reported that the rate of business incorporations in 1994 was 737,000—the highest in history. Independent entrepreneurs are becoming the downsized organization's external staff, hired to design or start up turnkey projects, such as integrating new computer systems, introducing workflow and imaging technologies, or developing new training and development systems. Researchers at Pepperdine University report that the average self-employed worker earns 40 percent more per hour than an employee, and that capital invested in one's own business pays high returns, compared with other investments (Mandel 1994, 89).

As an entrepreneur, you can manage projects in your areas of expertise for your former employer, while also working on projects with other clients. Becoming an entrepreneur can be an attractive option if you are prepared for the challenges.

> *One of the keys to having control of your life is having your own definition of success.*
>
> —Deborah Aguiar-Velez (Morris 1991, 29)

An example of an independent entrepreneur who continued to work with her former employer, as well as other clients, is Deborah Aguiar-Velez, founder and CEO of Sistemas Corporation, who left her job as a senior analyst at Exxon and started her own business, managing projects to develop customized computer software and training not only for Exxon but also for AT&T, Xerox, and others. She now embraces her new role, saying, "One of the keys to having control of your life is having your own definition of success" (Morris 1991, 29).

The *Wall Street Journal Report on Small Business* (Schellhardt 1996, R14) described these new entrepreneurs as playing a key role in the economy. Many are fleeing large corporations in increasing numbers, and at younger and younger ages, because they want to have more control over their lives and they want to see the results of their work. We maintain the new entrepreneurs will only achieve these goals, however, if they can learn to cope with change and risk.

If you are now, or plan to become, an entrepreneur, managing projects successfully will be an essential survival skill for you. You will need the skills to manage the output and functioning of your project teams and to manage the interactions with and expectations of the organizational units that sponsor your projects. You will also need to learn some successful strategies for dealing with incertainty, change, and risk.

What About Becoming an Intrapreneur?

You don't always need to go out on your own to be a project manager. The *Wall Street Journal Report on Small Business* (Schellhardt 1996, R14) described a different type of project manager—the *intrapreneur*. Some companies encourage employees to form project teams within the established organization to develop products or services that can increase the companies' business. This movement is the result of corporations' efforts to tap the creativity of their employees.

Companies such as IBM, AT&T, Dupont, Motorola, and the regional Bell companies provide resources to intrapreneurs to develop new products and services that expand their businesses. Intrapreneurs are allowed to exercise greater autonomy in designing new and creative approaches within the boundaries of the projects they design.

There are a number of examples of successful internal projects:

- *Thinx*, a graphics software program, was developed by a 20-person intrapreneur team at Bell Atlantic.
- A project team within IBM, because it could be located away from the corporate bureaucracy, which was committed to mainframes, was finally able to develop a personal computer to challenge industry competitors.
- At Chrysler, an intrapreneurial team designed and built the popular car Neon.
- At Minnesota Mining and Manufacturing, an intrapreneur developed the Post-it®.

If you are, or expect to be, an intrapreneur, you will face many of the same opportunities and risks as the independent entrepreneur and have the same need for project management skills.

Are You a New Technical Professional?

If you are, or soon expect to become, a highly credentialed graduate in almost any technical specialty, you are likely to be managing projects early in your career. You may discover that your college and professional training, whether in engineering, architecture, information technology, psychotherapy, or other fields, provided little information on how to apply those skills in managing projects. No matter how highly trained you are in your discipline, you will also need the skills to manage projects in an uncertain environment in which success involves solving complex problems, many of which do not respond to any of the textbook solutions you learned at school.

You will also have to prove yourself to clients. Karen Taylor (1996), production manager of Electronic Learning Facilitators (ELF), a multimedia production firm, says that their project managers are often very young. They typically have to establish credibility with the clients, particularly the more senior ones, by demonstrating quickly that they are highly knowledgeable about the technologies they are using and how those technlogies will help serve the client's needs, thus counteracting the first impression that ELF is entrusting the client's project to inexperienced employees. Conversely, if you are an older, career-changing technical degree graduate, you may have to overcome the initial reluctance of younger clients to work with a project manager across the generation gap. In either case, the project management skill related to customer and client relationships and communications will be even more critical than your technical expertise.

Are You the Leader of a Self-Managed Team?

You may work in an organization that has eliminated many middle management positions and given self-managed work teams responsibility for planning and decision making. For example, employee teams at Pitney Bowes identify work processes that need improvement and plan and execute projects to make those improvements. Projects are designed and managed by employee teams that meet on a regular basis, set goals, and develop plans to achieve those goals, using strategies learned through the company's team training programs. In speaking of these teams, Kevin Connolly of Pitney Bowes told *Business Week* (Farrell, Mandel, & Weber 1995, 146), "These workers make decisions all the time. Yet in the past, we treated them as if they were incapable of making decisions. . . . No more."

If you are leading a worker team, you will be able to apply the skills discussed in this book to cope with the uncertainty and risk that your team projects are likely to encounter.

Are You an Experienced Project Manager?

If, like the authors, you are one of the many beleaguered experienced project managers working in consulting, engineering, or other service functions that have traditionally been project environments, or managing projects that introduce imaging, workflow, or other information technologies, you probably are aware that conventional project management approaches aren't working for you. This book can provide you with some useful ideas gleaned from discussions with other project managers. The project managers we spoke with identified a variety of uncertainties that represent risks to their projects including:

- Technology changes that makes software obsolete.
- Budgets that become unrealistic, as clients demand changes to the work scope.
- Competition that forces prices down to the point at which a competitive price will not be high enough to result in a profit.
- Cash flow requirements that create pressure to ensure an immediate return on investment each month.
- Work scopes that keep changing (the dreaded "scope creep").
- Unanticipated reactions to project goals and outcomes.

We hope to convince you that these problems are not unique and that it is possible to manage projects successfully in the face of these and similar challenges.

Are You a Quality Professional?

If you are a quality professional, you have a major role in project management, even if you are not a project manager. You need to understand project management issues to be able to provide advice that will help project managers produce products and services of consistently high quality. Maintaining quality in the face of uncertainty and constantly changing requirements is your challenge. You will need to work with both the project team and the project sponsors to set quality standards and put systems in place to ensure that quality is not compromised as the project copes with change. Understanding the uncertainties and risks in project management can help you make useful recommendations to ensure that quality is not undermined.

In corporate organizations and government agencies, some project teams have been set up specifically to deal with quality issues. These projects may involve benchmarking efforts to identify organizations that are exemplars of high quality and from which your organization can gain knowledge and skills to improve the quality of your firm's products or services. As a quality professional managing such projects, you will face many of the challenges we describe in this book. You will have to gain support for the effort and overcome the negative attitudes of those who believe that an emphasis on quality takes time from other important areas. You will also have to combat the perception of total quality management as *last* month's flavor of the month.

More commonly, though, your role will be to provide advice and support to project managers, helping them to understand and communicate the quality standards of your organization and communicate them to their project staff. You can help project managers set up quality controls to ensure that the project outcomes satisfy customers and result in repeat business.

You may also need to educate project managers on your organization's commitment to ISO 9000 standards, and how these apply to products and services produced by their projects. Project managers may also need your help in understanding and applying such key quality measures as six sigma, statistical process control, and continuous improvement. You can give them tools to identify and eliminate non-value-added activity and to measure performance so that essential tasks are performed efficiently. You can keep project managers informed about both formal and on-the-job training available in the quality area and strengthen their ability to collect the data they need to prepare for internal or client quality audits.

In short, a quality professional has to be a missionary bent on improving quality standards throughout the organization. In today's highly matrixed organizations—in which most work is done through projects—that means you have a very useful role to play in focusing attention on quality issues.

Change and Uncertainty as the Universal Condition

Science affects the way we think together.

—Lewis Thomas

Lessons from Physical Science

Let's put the problem of uncertainty and constant change into a broader perspective. Science shows us that uncertainty and unpredictable change are major forces that govern the universe. So why shouldn't they impact project management?

Once, we were sure that we understood that electrons revolved around atoms in entirely predictable ways and that new information could fit logically into models we already understood. But as Carey and Dawley point out in *Business Week* (1996, 101), the discoveries of quantum physics overturned our cherished ideas about reality. Now we know that bits of matter can exist in more than one place at the same time and that electrons can pass through what seem impermeable walls. An electron can be a wave or a particle, and we can only tell what form it will take by actually observing it. These highly controversial findings were at first of interest only to theoretical physicists. However, practical applications of our understanding of subatomic particles and the theories of quantum physics are increasingly important. They have made possible the laser, the high-speed computer, the Boeing 777, and many other technological breakthroughs; and they have the potential to increase the storage capacity of a computer bit to 15,000 times what presently existing chips can store—a breakthrough sure to provide massive implications for computing and telecommunications.

Lessons from Natural Science

In the animal world, change has also been shown to be the norm—and adjusting to change the secret of survival. Evolutionary biologists Peter and Rosemary Grant (Weiner 1994, 249) observed the finches of the Galapagos Islands for over 20 years and found that birds evolve not over eons, as was formerly believed, but within a single generation. For example, the sizes of birds' beaks change in response to the available food supply. That is, there are always birds that can eat the larger or smaller nuts and seeds from whatever plants have survived such radical climate changes as floods or droughts.

The Message Received

How are these scientific discoveries relevant to project management? Scientific research and experience prove that uncertainty and rapid, continual change are natural phenomena and that survival demands rapid adaptation to inevitable change. These findings change and modify our understanding and use of the older sciences. This directly affects us as project managers because our well-entrenched theories of project management are grounded in Newtonian physics, and other rigid knowledge disciplines that have to be rethought as scientific information provides new and conflicting data.

Today's problems come from yesterday's solutions.

—Peter Senge (1990, 73)

David Meyers (1996), a highly respected project manager at Human Technology, Inc., points out that the rigid approach to project management had its origin with the generation of managers who were trained as military officers in World War II. These men (and they were almost exclusively men) received their management training in a traditionally hierarchical environment. They brought with them into the civilian business world the military philosophy that planning and controlling were the key management skills—a philosophy that assumes that the variances in a project can be known at the outset and controlled as they predictably arise.

But in today's world, reliance on planning and controlling does not, nor will not, make you a successful project manager. Our current understanding of reality requires new approaches that let us adapt to change and uncertainty. Meyers reminds us that, "If planning were the answer, the Soviet Union, with its penchant for long-range planning, would by now rule the world!"

Chapter 2

Managing Projects in a Quantum World

Project management without timelines and a budget is just a hobby.

—Beth Kamradt (1996)

In the conventional linear approach to project management, the project manager develops a work plan at the project start, establishing milestones for completion of project tasks. Estimates of labor, time, and other resources are made and a budget is developed, based on their anticipated cost. Once the plan and budget are approved, the project manager accepts responsibility for ensuring that project tasks are completed on time, and within budget, and that project deliverables meet quality standards. The high value placed on these activities is reflected in this chapter's opening quote from a project manager, who was working at the time of our interview at a major U.S. pharmaceutical company. Today, however, this linear approach seems to be out of control more than it is in control, because it cannot, and does not, take into account the constantly changing variables that can influence project progress.

The make-or-break issue is the unknown,
not the known.

—David Meyers (1996)

We are convinced that a new approach—a new paradigm—is needed to plan, implement, and complete projects in the face of uncertainty and the risk it engenders. Our experience, and that of the many other project managers we interviewed, is that projects rarely, if ever, proceed in the straightforward fashion dictated by traditional project management approaches. Rather, project plans must be constantly realigned over the life of the project to meet the changing demands of customers, to incorporate improvements in technology, and to constantly expand the knowledge and skills of the project team as these changes occur.

The Case of the Expanding/Shrinking Project

To put this in perspective, this fictional case study illustrates some of the changing demands and fluctuations that characterize project management today. Though it is imaginary, it combines aspects of uncertainty and risk that are common to many real-life projects—some painfully familiar to us, we regret to report. The experience of Joe Jones demonstrates the limits of the traditional project management approach. As you read about his experience, notice how uncertainty, change, and risk affected the outcomes of his project.

The Project

Joe Jones is project manager for the multimedia development firm, Multimedia Training Systems, Inc. (MTSI). MTSI has a contract with Dinner Out (DO), a local fast-food chain with 10 stores, to design a new-hire training program. The training is to be developed using multimedia on CD-ROM disks, and DO wants it in place as quickly as possible. Turnover at the DO stores is high, and training is a constant need.

The idea for this type of training arose when two DO headquarters managers saw a computer show demonstration of training that one of their competitors, a pizza chain, was using. The DO managers (from the human resources and purchasing departments) immediately decided they wanted similar training for their store employees. They felt that everything was in place for this type of training, since DO had recently purchased new computers with CD-ROM drives for all its stores. They were easily convinced that lessons on disk could replace traditional on-the-job employee training and free up the time that store managers had been spending on training. They were even more excited when they talked to a vendor of multimedia authoring software, who assured them that they or their secretaries could be creating multimedia within 15 minutes of loading their software.

DO chose MTSI to develop the training, because when these managers met Joe Jones at the same computer show, he told them that MTSI had developed CD-ROM-based training. The DO managers also liked a MTSI demo CD-ROM that Joe showed them.

The managers told Joe that they were very busy and did not have time to be involved in the training development. "We know our business, and you know your business. We've told you what we need. We need it as soon as you can finish it. Bring us a plan and we'll get it approved at headquarters. You can use our existing training manuals to get the content for the training disks."

Joe Jones was delighted. MTSI would have a free hand to develop a quality product and satisfy a new customer. He immediately developed a project plan and a budget.

Table 2-1 is the work plan Joe prepared. It shows the schedule of tasks to complete the project, the number of days each person is to spend on each task, the list of project deliverables, and the times to complete all the project deliverables within the six-month timeframe that the DO managers specified. The figures in the table show the staggered development approach and work dates that the team needs to use to get the project done on time.

Joe laid out a logical plan to complete the project within DO's six-month timeframe. He planned to contract with Alice, a well-qualified instructional designer experienced in designing multimedia training modules for CD-ROM; and with Pete, a highly experienced author/programmer who had worked on many computer-based training projects. Both were expensive, but they did top-quality work, and Joe felt he needed their level of experience to do the work as quickly as the customer wanted it.

The Plot Thickens

Several elements that typically interfere with project managers' plans now began to assume critical importance.

Stakeholders, Part 1

The day after Joe got his proposal approved by DO, he was told that managers from DO's marketing and sales departments would like to contribute to the planning of this project. Unlike the original managers (from human resources and purchasing) who had contracted with Joe, the sales and marketing managers were very interested in the details of the project and wanted to discuss what MTSI was planning. Joe, Alice, and Pete, had several lengthy meetings with these new participants to discuss the project scope and coverage.

Task	Deliverables	Work Dates	Due Dates	Project Manager	Instructional Designer	Pro-grammer	Word Processor Editor	Total Days
Collect and review existing materials		Weeks 1 & 2		3	2		1	6
Collect additional pertinent information		Weeks 1 & 2		3	3	3		9
Develop training module design map	Training module design map	Weeks 2 & 3	End Week 3	1	8	5	3	17
DO review of design map	Approved design map	Week 4	End Week 4	1	1	1		3
Draft storyboards of training modules	Programmable storyboards	Staggered Weeks 5-17	End Week 17	6	15 (5@3)		2	23
Author training modules	Programmed modules	Staggered Weeks 6-18	End Week 18	6		15 (5@3)	2	23
Internal review of modules	Edited modules	Staggered Weeks 6-18	End Week 18	1	2	2	4	9
Conduct in-store tests of modules	Completed field tests	Staggered Weeks 8-19	Week 19	1	4 (5@.75)	4 (5@.75)		9
Revise modules and prepare documentation	Final modules/ documentation	Weeks 20 & 21	Week 21	1	5	4	1	13
Produce CD-ROMs	CD-ROMs	Weeks 22 & 23	Week 23			2	1	3
Install in stores	Installed training	Week 24	Week 24	1		3		4
TOTAL EST. DAYS				24	40	40	15	119

Table 2-1. Work Plan, Deliverable Schedule, and Labor Allocation

> ➤ *The Risk: New stakeholders, escalating labor costs, expanding time requirements.*

Training Content, Part 1

The sales and marketing managers immediately pointed out that the existing training manuals could not provide the training content for the CD-ROM, because they were five years old and didn't include the new DO food items and customer awards that sales and marketing were anxious to have employees promote with customers.

> ➤ *The Risk: Data not available according to project assumptions.*

Stakeholders, Part 2

Joe and the project team visited the stores and found, to their surprise, that most of the store managers had not been consulted about the training and were unwilling to cooperate with the project. Their ideas about employee training had not been sought before the contract had been given to MTSI. Several store managers told the project team that they much preferred to train employees one-on-one, by personally showing them how to do each task. This gave them a chance to get to know their employees. "Besides, one manager said, "our people are seldom literate enough to read manuals. It's much easier to just tell them what to do." When asked about the possibility of using computers for training, neither the managers nor the new hires seemed comfortable with the idea. "If these people could use computers, why would they be working *here*?" one manager asked Joe.

In fact, several of the store managers believed that the reason headquarters wanted to provide multimedia training was to justify the recent purchase of high-powered computers for the stores, which the store managers said they did not need. They saw the training idea as a smoke screen to provide a justification for this "needless" purchase. Although some resistance and doubt were expected, the project team was shocked by the extent of the gap between headquarters' expectations and those of the store managers and employees.

> ➤ *The Risk: End-user resistance, rejection of project goals.*

The Technology

Naturally, the project team was interested in seeing the new computers to make sure they were configured and placed appropriately for the proposed training. However, this presented another problem. Although the computers had been ordered, none had yet been delivered to the stores. The different store managers did point out the spaces they could make available to house the new computers. Space was at a premium at all the stores, and the computers would have to be set up in crowded, cluttered, noisy spaces in or behind the kitchens—very poor environments for training.

> ➤ *The Risk: Physical environment not conducive to the intended technology use.*

Training Content, Part 2

Back at her office, Alice reviewed the existing DO training manuals. She could see that they were out of date, based on what she had observed the store employees doing. Even if they had covered the necessary tasks, the content in the manuals did not provide enough information to fully develop the training material for the CD-ROM. She would need to spend several days at the stores interviewing employees and managers to find out more about the job tasks and the new products being offered in the stores to be able to define what should be included in the training.

> *The Risk: Labor costs escalating beyond the project budget.*

Rescoping by MTSI

Joe Jones now faced a critical dilemma. The contract he had agreed to could not be carried out. The scope and coverage of the project had changed. The target population had different skills and experience than he had predicted. Additional work would be required. The promised project products could not be delivered in the timeframe and at the cost agreed upon. Joe had no choice but to begin redoing his budget and project plan before he had received any payment.

> *The Risk: Project costs accumulating without an agreed-upon contract.*

The Competition

Just at this point, a family-owned carryout, serving delicious food at lower prices than DO, opened across from DO's busiest store. DO profits fell dramatically. All attention at DO became focused on how to deal with this new threat.

> *The Risk: Shift in DO priorities due to unanticipated competitive threat.*

Rescoping by DO

DO told MTSI that they had to focus their resources on dealing with this competition. They asked MTSI to complete the training project in half of the originally scheduled time and at half the agreed-upon price.

> *The Risk: The project cannot be viable, given the funding and time available.*

The Uncertainty Principle at Work

No problem can be solved from the same consciousness that created it. We must learn to see the world anew.

—Albert Einstein

In chapter 1 we said that uncertainty is the driving force in our universe. The fictional MTSI case and the many, many real-world situations it is based on show clearly that this is not just a theoretical notion, but the realistic challenge of project management. Cases like Joe's provide proof of the quantum physicist's conclusion that observation and interaction create reality. We cannot model reality in a project context by drawing charts and timetables. We need a model that allows us to anticipate and adjust to uncertainty and change.

Sources of Uncertainty and Risk

In most projects. uncertainty and the risks associated with it will usually be related to one of the forces that drives contemporary work—that is, business needs of the organization, stakeholder goals, technology, and competition (or other environmental factors).

Let's look at how each of these forces actually impacted this project.

Business Needs of the Organization. DO management told MTSI that training was their priority goal. However, the truth was that making a profit was their most critical business need. This had to be their first priority. Closely related priorities were maintaining their customer base and attracting new customers. Thus, when the new family restaurant threatened their profits, improved training became a lower priority.

Stakeholder Goals. The individual goals of the store managers were crucial to the success of the project, but these were not known to Joe when he planned the project. Store managers were totally convinced that the best way to improve employees' performance was for the manager to be personally involved in their training. Managers also used the training to identify high-potential new recruits who could quickly take on responsibility for the stores, allowing the managers time to do ordering and other administrative work—not to mention see more of their families.

The store managers also did not want the headache of maintaining the high-priced computer equipment and the computer-based training materials. The training manuals had been enough of a problem—they had become obsolete within a year—and the managers expected the same to be true of the computer-based training materials. Managers felt that training was an important task that only they could do, because they kept abreast of DO's promotions and products, which had to change constantly to keep customers interested.

Technology. The DO headquarters managers who contracted with MTSI based their expectations for the training project on the capabilities of CD-ROM technology to meet their organizational training needs, as they saw them. They were convinced that sitting employees in front of a computer screen would free store managers from the burden of training and would leave them more time to devote to other details of the business. The new state-of-the-art computers—headquarters' latest attempt to upgrade DO stores' technology—would quickly pay for themselves. Packaging the training on CD-ROM would ensure that training would be identical at all stores, creating employees who could be assigned to any store location without the need for additional training.

Competition. DO expected the training to make their operation more competitive by making more efficient use of store managers' time. Their training would be as good as the training program of a pizza chain whose products were very popular in the neighborhoods where DO operated restaurants. Store managers, relieved of training responsibilities, could devote more time to greeting customers, identifying their needs, dealing with vendors on price and delivery problems, and making their stores more attractive than their competitors'. DO did not anticipate that a greater threat would come from a new restaurant that they had not known would be opening in their area.

Wicked Problems

The ability to identify and work toward what is desired rather than away from what is undesired or feared needs careful cultivation. We have a great deal of experience with the latter and very little good experience with the former.

— Harold Nelson (1994, 25)

Harold Nelson says that the trouble with using a problem-solving approach is that there is a problem with problems. Nelson, quoting Horst Rittel (1972), points out that there are two basic kinds of problems: *tame* problems and *wicked* problems. Joe Jones was faced with a wicked problem, but he used the following steps, which are only effective for solving tame problems:

1. Define the problem.
2. Gather information.

3. Analyze the infolmation.
4. Generate solutions.
5. Select the best solution.
6. Implement the best solution.
7. Test the solution.
8. Revise as needed.

Joe planned his project using this rational approach. Wicked problems, however, don't respond to standard analytical approaches, with prescribed outcomes. They require a holistic, intuitive, nonrational approach that looks much more deeply into the situation and identifies and involves everyone who has a stake in the outcomes. Nelson suggests that this proactive design approach will lead to better outcomes, especially for those projects involving organizational change.

Joe needed to take a collaborative approach that would involve DO managers and decision makers in the project planning. He didn't do that because he was intent on his personal desire to do the project and because the enthusiasm of his original contacts with DO gave him the false confidence that he could accomplish the work without their becoming involved. Had he insisted on being given an opportunity to get to know everyone who had an interest in the project—the store managers, the sales and marketing managers, the store employees, and perhaps others—he probably could have designed a more realistic project approach. Only after he submitted his proposal did he learn that there were uncertainties related to each of these important questions:

- What is the problem to be solved or the product to be created?
- What is the expected result from solving the problem or creating the product?
- Who are the parties concerned about it?

- Who will make decisions about resolving the problem?
- Whose performance is expected to be affected by the project outcomes?
- What resources are actually available for the project?
- What support will be available to implement the project?
- Given the answers to these questions, how should the organization proceed?

Joe's initial response to the changed situation was to rework his charts, develop a new budget based on the additional time required to research the training content, develop a new deliverables schedule, and reallocate the labor within the shorter timeframe available. In the sample project, this approach would fail totally, because it would not integrate the many interrelated aspects of this project. It would bypass the critical differences between headquarters and store managers on the fundamental question of what problem the training is intended to solve. It would overlook the important point that a training strategy that is appropriate for a competitor firm is not necessarily right for DO.

Instead of the project plan shown in Table 2-1, which was built around fixed times and deliverable specifications, Joe needs a project plan built around desired outcomes and more flexible delivery specifications and dates. His plan should build in continuous feedback from the various project stakeholders, so that as new information brings to light another bit of uncertainty or change from what was previously known, Joe and his project clients can use it to make credible decisions about updating the plan.

Another Approach—The Army's VUCA

To manage projects successfully with incomplete answers to the critical questions we've identified requires the project manager to get the best answers possible and then build into the project plan the capability to continually reassess and modify the original design concept to cope with the uncertainties and risks involved. Joe saw the project as a straightforward effort, culminating in the production of a CD-ROM training program. His project design did not account for the technical, political, social, communications, and professional aspects that were crucial to the success of the project.

It is interesting to note that although the approach Joe was following comes from an earlier military model, the U.S. Army today is rethinking this model. Army Chief of Staff Gen. Gordon Sullivan told *Fortune* magazine that he wants his officers to model themselves on the improvisational style of jazz musicians like Wynton Marsalis, who respond to other players in real time, rather than following a predetermined score. Sullivan has coined the acronym *VUCA* for the uncertain world the Army faces today—that is, **Violent, but also Uncertain, Complex and Ambiguous** (Smith 1994, 212).

> *You saw vehicles upright one minute and then nose-down the next. Nobody ever saw anything like this in training.*
>
> —U.S. Army Sergeant Carlos J. Tillman (Spolar 1995, A1)

The truth of General Sullivan's prediction that improvisation would be critical to contemporary Army missions was evident in the Army's recent project to ford the Sava River with a one-lane pontoon bridge to enter Bosnia. Called in as a peace-making force, the Army anticipated the potential for troops to be caught in crossfire if previously warring parties relapsed into hostility. But as the Army began preparation for 20,000 troops to cross, it encountered not military aggression, but a swollen river that, reaching flood levels not seen in 100 years, submerged the bridges, flooded tents and encampments, and made it necessary to build not one conventional bridge, but two bridges by dropping pontoon sections from helicopters (Spolar 1995, A1 and A27).

In the town, a local resident who lives at the river's edge told a reporter that she had been watching from her front yard with interest. "The waters have been coming halfway up this hill for the past two years," she said with a grin. The local head of the water authority, asked about the American's decision to camp by the river, said he had not been consulted in advance and expressed surprise at the Army's choice of a crossing point. Army officials said they had relied on statistical and satellite information. Fortunately for this project, additional resources were available to deal with the uncertainties in this situation; only time and effort were lost (items most of us cannot afford to lose).

The FAA Advanced Automation System

Project failures caused by wicked problems and the VUCA real world can occur in projects, both large and small. One that is of major interest for you if you do much business travel, and that has major implications on an international scale, is the FAA Advanced Automation System (AAS), a project intended to modernize the national airspace. The project involves providing 7,000 new controller consoles for a system that would have a reliability of no more than two seconds per year of downtime.

> ➤ *The Risk: Potentially unattainable goal.*

Planning began in the early 1980s, and the project finally got underway in 1988, when after protracted legal challenges, the contract to build the system was awarded to IBM. Like the MTSI manager in our imaginary project, in this real-life, critical project, the sponsor, FAA, gave IBM functional specifications and a free hand to design a new system. The

FAA's Robert Valone, lecturing at Catholic University (1994), said that because the FAA did not have the management expertise in software and hardware engineering, business management, or systems engineering to monitor this complex project, it relied on IBM to supply these, with minimal FAA oversight.

➤ *The Risk: Lack of expertise to manage a complex project.*

However, as IBM began to complete designs and prototype them, they found that, in fact, the users of the system—the Air Traffic Controllers (ATCs)—who, like the sales and marketing managers at DO, had not been consulted when the headquarters staff wrote the functional specifications for the contract, nor when the contractor developed the proposal—could and did reject the designs. IBM found that the project requirements could not be stabilized because controllers said the designs were unsuited to the ATC work environment. Thus, the failure to involve these stakeholders early in the design stage resulted in constant design changes, which triggered massive cost overruns.

➤ *The Risk: Uncertainty of user acceptance.*

Because the FAA had been unwilling to choose from available commercial software vendor products, IBM had to agree to develop the approximately 5 million lines of programming code needed in Ada, a computer language developed and owned by the Department of Defense. However, IBM found it did not have programmers experienced with Ada. Ada also had few of the development tools that speed up programming, which would have been available for more widely used commercial languages, such as C.

➤ *The Risk: Inappropriate technology.*

As the multiyear project continued, personal computers, workstations, multimedia, graphical user interface environments, motion, color, sound, and interactivity became available to make computer systems more efficient and user-friendly; but these innovations could not be incorporated into the inflexible project design. In addition, when the cold war ended, and the Defense Department allowed the restricted use of its Global Positioning Satellites for commercial use, offering entirely new approaches to controlling air traffic, these changes in the technology state of the art could not be incorporated.

Delays in software development eventually led to so many cost overruns and missed delivery dates that by 1994, the project was $3 billion in the red. This caused a lack of confidence on the part of the FAA's funding sources in Congress. Hearings were held, and the press and the aviation industry continued to complain about the project delays. Loral replaced IBM as prime contractor. By 1994, the *Washington Post* was describing the project as "a broad-scale retreat . . . from one of the most ambitious computer modernization projects undertaken by the U.S. government" (Weintraub 1994, B1). The budgeted cost of the project when the contract was let to IBM in 1988 was $4.3 billion. As of June 4, 1994, the Government Accounting Office (U.S. GAO 1994) reported that the FAA's cost estimate to complete the work was about $7 billion, and that was for a much-reduced effort designed to complete only the most critical elements of the project.

➤ *The Risk: Eroding stakeholder support.*

In 1996, this project continues to be mired in controversy, and it probably will not be completed for many more years. A blue ribbon panel reported to the FAA in January 1996 that 23 power outages at ATC facilities had shut down controllers' computers and phones and caused massive airline delays. The panel reported that ATC centers' computers are now 25 years old. "Technicians are reluctant to complete scheduled periodic maintenance," because some equipment is so old and the wiring is so brittle. Where new equipment is being installed, electricians either have not been trained to maintain it or they were trained years ago and have forgotten what they learned.

FAA oversight remains a problem. The ATC centers complained to the panel that FAA headquarters cannot provide time to resolve issues as they come up (Mintz 1996).

This contemporary project illustrates clearly the need for a new, flexible approach to project management. For example, the project goals in 1988 were simple, reflecting the environment of the cold war, the minimal concern with global competition, and a focus on doing existing processes more efficiently. The original goals reflected scant interest in either the airline industry or the public as stakeholders. The 1988 goals were:

- Upgrade the ATC technology.
- Improve controller productivity.

The FAA's goals today reflect the new era of deregulation and global competition with an FAA focus on service to the citizens and the competitive challenge to U.S. commercial aviation. Todays goals are to:

- Improve service to airline travelers.
- Save fuel and shorten flight times.
- Make the U.S. airline industry the most competitive in the world.

➤ *The Risk: Changing project goals.*

The Need for a New Approach to Project Management

Reality is made up of circles but we see straight lines.

—Peter Senge (1990, 73)

The fictional multimedia project and the all-too-real Army and FAA projects encompass many of the characteristics that convince us that a new approach to project management is necessary—one that incorporates the flexibility to accept uncertainty and change as inevitable. In project management, as in quantum physics, reality is created by being able to observe and react to the interactions among all the stakeholders and the changing influences of the environments in which individuals and their organizations operate.

Senge (1990) says we need to adjust our perspective, from seeing linear cause-and-effect relationships, to seeing how the many interrelationships at work in a situation will affect the outcomes. He advises us to move from seeing a series of snapshots, to seeing a series of change processes and realizing that they will have uncertain outcomes.

In chapter 3 we introduce a new approach for dealing with wicked problems and the uncertainty they create, and in the chapters that follow we describe the strategies and tools that will help project managers recognize these wicked problems and deal effectively with the uncertainty and risk they produce.

A New Project Management Approach

What we anticipate seldom occurs; what we least
expected generally happens.

—Benjamin Disraeli

Overview

Project managers we have talked with, whatever their field and regardless of the size or type of project they managed, have agreed that the uncertainties in project management make the traditional linear approaches unrealistic and that a new approach is needed. They said this in a variety of ways:

The make-or-break issue is the unknown, not the known.

—Dave Meyers (1996)

You need to build in nightmare time—though you never know when you'll need it—it's different on every project.

—Karen Taylor (1996)

If the old project management models don't work, what can replace them?

41

This chapter lays out an approach for planning and managing projects that the authors believe will work more effectively than the currently used linear approaches. Our model shares some of the characteristics and strategies of previously used models, but it embraces as its two organizing principles that:

- All project goals, objectives, and environments change from the beginning of the project to the end of the project.
- All stakeholders influence and in fact change the project as they work on it, review its products, and implement its results.

This project management approach recognizes the absolute certainty that uncertainty will frame and produce many of the project processes, outputs, and results. It also builds in ongoing risk assessment to help you identify and come to grips with that uncertainty before it overwhelms you.

Breaking Out of the Boxes

March is when the year is annually created anew,
and that is when the calendar of the soul begins.

—Joseph Wood Krutch (1949)

Krutch thought that the year should begin in March, rather than in January, because for gardeners and other nature lovers, March is the month richest in anticipation. We believe this is exactly the attitude and vision you should embrace at the start of each new project. It is a time to explore and dream and create wonderful visions of what is to come. It is also the time to set the stage for all that comes next. It is your opportunity to recast or rearrange the current environment to help bring about that new vision. To do this sometimes requires an entirely new outlook concerning your environment and new ways of defining the beginning and ending point to your year. Gardeners, architects, engineers, and artists all have implicit faith that their visions can be achieved, regardless of the obstacles. Project managers need that same faith and belief in the possible.

Consider the following two statements:

- Project management is a fallacy, a myth, a recurring and persistent dream of people who've been placed in the unenviable role of being in charge of a project.
- Project management is a challenge, an exhilarating process, an opportunity to create a different way of doing things and produce new results.

What is the difference between these statements? Attitude. This attitude difference is one of the main features in the project management approach we are proposing. If you believe that project management is about choosing and using the right organization and time and cost control methods, we predict you will fail to achieve your objectives. We have found that fixed, rigid, predefined ways of controlling project processes and components get in the way of—rather than help in—achieving project goals and results.

We believe instead that project management is about enabling people to work together to construct creative solutions that make sense for the organization and environment in which they operate. This requires using a flexible approach and adaptable methods for dealing with the uncertainty and changeability of the situation and the environment. Our model, which uses traditional project management tools where they are useful, has at its core an attitude of flexibility, discovery, risk assessment, and sense-checking throughout the project life cycle. It requires that the project manager embrace uncertainty and risk as givens, rather than as foes that can be tricked into submission or defeat. If you and your project team believe in the project and its goal, and are willing to adapt your processes throughout the project, you can and will succeed. You just have to have faith and be willing to bend a bit along the way. And that is what our model helps you do.

New Approach in Brief

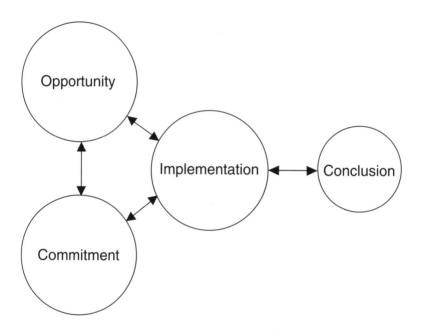

Figure 3-1. Project Management Stages

Our project management model, shown in Figure 3-1, is based on four interactive sets of activities, or stages, that are triggered by a problem or opportunity.

- The opportunity stage is when the goals and critical success factors of the project are determined.
- The commitment stage is when the necessary resources are pulled together into a work approach that is agreed to by all of the project stakeholders.

- The implementation stage is when the actual project work is completed according to the agreed-upon goals and resource plans.
- The conclusion stage is the final set of activities done to complete the project and to make the transition to normal work activities.

A project is usually begun in the opportunity stage with the identification of a problem to solve or an opportunity to seek. Activities in the commitment stage start soon thereafter, particularly when resources (e.g., staff, time, and money) are needed to complete the analyses of the opportunity stage. Implementation stage activities normally do not begin until the intial project scoping and analysis activities of the opportunity stage are completed and all of the project planning and specification activities of the commitment stage are done and resources are secured.

Activities during each of the first three stages affect the activities and conclusions in the other two, so regular interactions and feedback loops are built in to make sure that the project stays on track throughout its life cycle. The conclusion stage mainly interacts with the implementation stage activities as work on the various project elements is done. At any point, uncertainty and change can cause the direction of the project to change or the force of the movement to alter. An alert project manager should recognize these triggers and take immediate action to minimize the risks of continuing the project activities as planned. This may require adjustments to the vision and goals stated in the opportunity stage, or to the resource commitments made in the commitment stage, or to the configurations or planned activities of the work teams in the implementation stage. Failure to recognize that relationships and interactions always change original ideas and plans is fatal to the ultimate success of any project.

At each stage of a project you and the project team will primarily be trying to answer the questions shown in Table 3-1.

Table 3-1. Primary Project Questions by Stage

Stage	Questions
Opportunity	• What are we trying to accomplish? • How will we know we accomplished what we set out to do?
Commitment	• How do we get from here to there?
Implementation	• How do we define, build, and test our ideas? • How do we deploy the ideas?
Conclusion	• How do we know when we are done?

Nested within the implementation stage is a spiraling set of activities (see Figure 3-2) that work to achieve the project goal. This part of the model is an adaptation of the spiral

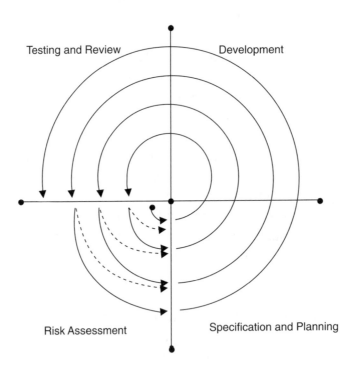

Figure 3-2. Project Management Implementation Stage Spirals

models described by Boehm; deHoog, et. al.; and Banathy (Boehm 1988; deHoog, et.al. 1994; Banathy 1994). It combines and collapses the analysis, design, development, and testing phases of the traditional systems development waterfall model (shown in Figure 3-3) into successive spirals of product or solution development. Each of these spirals incorporates risk assessment, specification and planning, development, and testing and review. Each spiral is a mini-project in itself, encompassing all the activities needed to complete a particular element or deliverable of the project as a whole. Built into each spiral is a set of activities that helps you to determine the risks of proceeding and then to select the correct strategy and direction to proceed based on those risks.

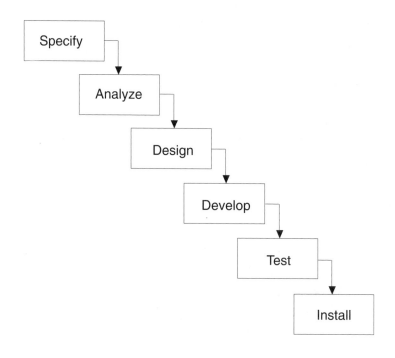

Figure 3-3. Traditional Systems Development Waterfall Model

Our model differs from the traditional systems development waterfall model in that it:

- Assumes uncertainty and change as a natural part of any project.
- Adds flexibility to traditional systems development methodologies.
- Encourages the integration of project methodology, product output, and development tools throughout project.
- Encourages a rapid prototyping or successive approximation product design and development approach.
- Uses an interactive process for reassessing the project intent and current risk so that any necessary adaptations to the project process and product can be made along the way.
- Assumes that a project manager alone cannot, and should not, try to control the project in isolation, without full and conscious participation of all of the project stakeholders.
- Acknowledges the reality that all projects exist within a larger environment that can and will affect the project throughout its life cycle.

The following sections offer more detailed discussion of each of the stages and spirals in our model to help make these abstract concepts real.

Opportunity Stage

"Would you tell me, please, which way I have to go from here?" Alice asked. "That depends a good deal on where you want to get to," said the cat. "I don't much care where," said Alice. "Then it doesn't matter which way you go," said the cat.

—Lewis Carroll

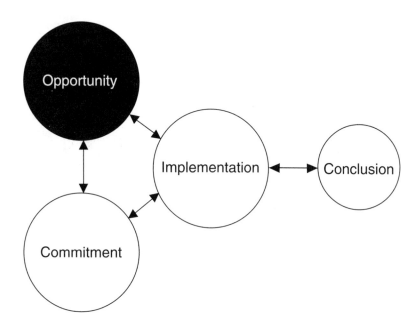

Figure 3-4. Project Management Stages: Opportunity

This is the most important stage of any project the development of a detailed definition of the problem or opportunity
being tackled by the project, the project scope, and the design
concept. This is the "where you want to get to" that Alice did-
n't much care about—a place you should and do care about,
very much. The result of this stage of activities should provide the general context and specific information necessary
to answer the questions, What are we trying to accomplish?,
What do we want to have happen as a result?, and How will
we know we accomplished what we set out to do? Without
detailed answers to these questions, and the others shown in
Table 3-2, you will be unable to identify the uncertainty and
risks that may prevent you from effectively planning and
managing the project. You may end up planning a project to
accomplish something very different from what you should
be trying to accomplish.

Table 3-2. Questions to Resolve: Opportunity Stage

Type of Analysis	Questions
Problem definition	1. What are you (is the project) trying to do? 2. What do you expect to happen as a result? 3. How will you know when you get there?
Problem and impact	4. What problem or opportunity do you hope to solve or exploit? 5. What is the impact on the organization if the problem or threat is not resolved? 6. What is the impact on the organization if the opportunity is not exploited?

Stakeholder	7. Who are the stakeholders and what are their roles and expectations in the project?
	   a. Who initiated the project?
	   b. Who is the project's major sponsor and why does this person think the project is necessary?
	   c. Who is the project team's customer?
	   d. Who are the end users of the project's products and services?
	   e. Who will make decisions and sign off on project products and services?
	8. What is the sponsor's level and quality of commitment and amount of fiscal support?

Organizational and cultural assessment	9. Does the organization see and understand the need for this project? 10. Is the organization ready and capable of dealing with this project and the changes it will entail?
Alternative solution and risk assessment	11. What are possible alternative ways of approaching or constructing the project solutions or outputs (in terms of design concept, technology architecture, and physical configuration)? 12. What are the cost savings and return on investment (ROI) potential for each alternative? 13. What are the risks associated with each of the possible solutions given the current environment and the current organizational structure and culture?

Value	14. Is the project worth doing?
	15. What are the most significant aspects to track during the project?
	   a. Financial?
	   b. Organizational?
	   c. Technical?
	   d. Competitive/marketing environment?

Project scope and definition	16. What should be the specific project purpose, scope, and objectives? 17. What critical success factors should be used to determine whether to stop or continue the project at each project cycle? 18. What will a successful outcome look like to the client? To you? To your team?

This confusion about project goals was an issue for Lori in one of her first major projects. The originally stated project goal was to convert some classroom training into computer-based training (CBT) that could be taken in local offices in order to reduce training travel and per diem costs associated with classes at regional training centers. A simple training conversion project, right? However, initial analysis of the problem showed the project team that an opportunity existed to reduce total training time and improve training and resulting job performance results by redesigning of the curriculum to incorporate a variety of alternative training methods and integrated on-the-job activities. The improved training could, in fact, get new trainees to the job "faster, cheaper, and better" (Gillespie and Budd 1984). And even though it didn't run exactly as planned, the redefined project led to savings that far exceeded the initial project goals—despite a hefty up-front cost for equipment, software, and materials development. The point is, many problems are in reality opportunities. The trick is to define and analyze the project in such a way that permits a full exploration of the problem and any potential opportunities that might arise. Conversely, if your project is exploring a new opportunity, you need to analyze it in such a way as to identify any related problems that it might engender. If Lori's project team had not discovered the other possible opportunities, they risked the loss of a substantial amount of savings and the very real possibility that the project would have created an incorrect solution to the stated problem.

Opportunity Stage Tasks and Activities

The opportunity stage can and should be thought of as a mini-project in itself. It creates the foundation upon which all the rest of the project is built. It is a time for both creative visioning and practical organization. As the project manager, you want to find out as much as possible about the environment and organizational milieu that has led to this project, including people's feelings about it. Not only do you need to define the project and expected result in great detail, but you also need to find out where the barriers (and skeletons) lie; what carrots are available to lure people toward progress; what the real goals, expectations, and critical success factors for the project process and products are; what the risks are; and what the potential return on investment is.

Table 3-3. Opportunity Stage Tasks and Activities

✔	Tasks
	1. Develop the project vision, mission, and goals.
	2. Get commitment to the vision, mission, and goals from all stakeholders.
	3. Define and analyze the problem or threat and its impact and/or conduct creative visioning of the opportunity and its impact.
	4. Describe and analyze the stakeholders.
	5. Assess the organizational culture in terms of change readiness and capability and the level of internal and external dissatisfaction with the current situation.
	6. Determine possible alternatives for solution of the problem or threat or exploitation of the opportunity.
	7. Conduct risk and cost analysis of the problem, threat, or opportunity and possible solutions given the current organizational culture.
	8. Decide if the project is worth doing.
	9. On the basis of previous analyses, specify the immediate project purpose, scope and objectives, and critical success factors (and relate them to general intermediate and long-term goals for the project and related organizational efforts).
	10. Make go/no go project decision and set decision parameters for stopping or continuing at the end of each project cycle.
	11. Identify the trade-offs to complete a quality job in the time available.

You should plan activities in the opportunity stage to create an ever more detailed picture of the project vision and goals, from the point of view of all its affected stakeholders. A list of some of the typical kinds of activities done in this stage is shown in Table 3-3. Completing these tasks is an iterative process that produces many fuzzy first drafts of the vision. The final picture may bear only a slight resemblance to the idea that started the project, but that is all right. That should indicate that you got input and information from more that one source, thereby creating a more complete, fully formed picture, or blueprint, from which to proceed.

Most of the activities in this stage are related to data gathering and analysis. You will be looking for data to support the project need. For example: Is the data convincing or persuasive to the sponsor? Who has the data? Was the data obtained from interviews with experts? From discussions with other project managers? From on-line searches (e.g., of LEXIS, NEXIS, or the Internet)? From other business sources? Is there enough data to make a judgment about the potential value of the expected project outcomes? Is it convincing? How credible is the source? Have any similar projects already been done? What were the results?

From these data you are creating a feasibility study, a paper prototype if you will, of the project vision. You are also testing and modifying the idea. On the basis of the results of your analyses, you should be able to clearly:

- Define the specific project purpose and objectives.
- Delineate the project scope boundaries.
- Identify the critical success factors that will be used to track project progress and product completion.
- Describe what a successful outcome will look like to each of the project stakeholders.

Failure to get a clear, integrated picture of that project vision and project goals will lead you into a complex maze, much as Alice found herself in Wonderland.

Risk Assessment

During the opportunity stage you identify the primary areas of uncertainty that you face in the project. In addition you should uncover some ideas about how to mitigate the risks associated with those areas of uncertainty within the course of your analysis activities. For example, one of the biggest areas of uncertainty for information systems-related projects is technology. If you have a technology-based vision, you will need to ask such questions as:

- Is there a technology available to help solve this problem?
- Is it the right one?
- How close is it to being ready to use?
- What happens if some new technology emerges some time during the project that might solve the problem better?

Uncertainty identification and risk mitigation start in the opportunity stage. Make sure you and all the project stakeholders are clear about the risks involved before you commit resources to the continuation of the project. Otherwise, don't be surprised when you start seeing signs that say "this way there be dragons" as you attempt to continue with the project.

Organizational Example

The General Accounting Office (GAO), the federal government agency that conducts audits of agencies and their programs for Congress, has developed a project management model to deal with the uncertainties in their environment.

Before they begin a project in response to a request from Congress, they convene a team to review the profile of the agency they have been requested to audit. They review its mission statements, organizational structure, contracts in progress, and databases. They ask:

- Why is this issue important?
- How does it relate to our other priorities or lines of effort?
- What methodology or approach will be used?

- What are the time and cost requirements likely to be?
- Will the project open new avenues to develop expertise or offer unique staff development opportunities?

GAO has developed a tool called the design matrix to document and internally communicate its design to stakeholders. As the project design becomes clearer, the design matrix becomes the team's internal communication vehicle. GAO then brings the stakeholders together to reach decisions on the job design, key milestone dates, and cost estimates. At the conclusion of this design summit, the team has a completed final design matrix, using the form shown in Figure 3-5.

For example, GAO received a request from Congress to review White House pass and security clearance procedures, to determine whether some White House staff did not have permanent passes or security clearances after being in the White House for over a year.

The top half of the design matrix in Figure 3-5 outlines the front-end analysis of the job. They begin with a job screening stage, asking, Is this the job to do? (i.e., compared with other potential jobs awaiting GAO action). GAO often negotiates with the requester about priorities during this stage. Once the decision is made to go ahead, the project moves into a job acceptance stage. A team is formed to work on it, stakeholders are identified, time and costs to complete are identified, and GAO and the customer reach agreement on the project plan. The stakeholders identified in this case are the White House and Secret Service officials and employees working in the White House. The GAO team prepares a design matrix, and a letter of intent is sent to the customer, outlining GAO's intention to undertake the job and committing GAO to provide a specific product by a certain date. In this case, the letter included the specific job objectives, the scope and methodology, the type of product to be prepared, the delivery date, and an agreed-upon schedule for

Design Matrix for [Insert review name]
Job Code [Insert job code]

Issue/Problem
[Insert brief description of problem]

Research Question	Information Required	Information Sources	Overall Design Strategy	Data Collection Methods	Data Analysis Methods	Limitations	What the analysis will allow you to say
[Insert questions to be reached]	[Summarize information requirements for addressing major questions]	[Summary description of information sources]	[Summarize overall design strategy by major issue]	[Summarize data collection methods by major issue]	[Summarize the data analysis methods to be used]	[Describe in summary form any limitations in the analysis]	[Summarize conclusions to be derived from the analysis]

Key Milestones and Dates:
[Summarize key milestones/dates derived from plans]

Costs (Rounded to the nearest $10,000):
[Summarize costs by major cost centers and subprocesses;
for example, headquarters/region costs by data collection report processing phases]

Figure 3-5. GAO Design Matrix

meeting and communicating with the customer. The front-end analysis ends when the project enters the commitment stage.

The bottom half of the design matrix is a work plan that outlines the steps to be carried out and the requirements of each step and concludes with the issuance of the GAO report, after appropriate reviews and approvals are completed. In the case of the White House passes, GAO provided a detailed plan for obtaining background information on the process and analyzing timeframes for pass and clearance processes. The plan outlined the schedule for examining available documentation and identified people to be interviewed. Using the data collected, GAO then prepared a report for approval by the appropriate issue area, provided the report to the stakeholders for review, and published and distributed the report.

The completed design matrix serves as the documentation of the opportunity stage (top half) and the commitment stage (bottom half). The final report generated from the data collected during the implementation stage as planned in the commitment stage is the final deliverable of the project.

Who's Involved in the Opportunity Stage?

The key to future success is to get buy-in and commitment at the project start from the important decision makers and the parts of the organization that will be affected. Involving these key people and their representatives in the opportunity stage is needed to get ultimate project acceptance; so by all means, involve them now. Does this mean you must wait until everyone can participate in this process before the project can begin? Not necessarily. It just means that you will need to keep trying throughout the project to find ways to involve the missing people and communicate the progress and results of the project to them as you go along. This can be done in several ways, depending on the situation and the project resources. You can send invitations to all stakeholders—not just the ones directly involved—to attend briefings on the project progress, following up with a telephone call to make sure they come. You can also keep them informed through newsletters, e-mail messages, and frequent telephone calls and drop-in visits. Add previously noninvolved stakeholders later during succesive spirals of the implementation stage to the teams of people doing, testing, and reviewing. Make sure that people do not feel the project is going on behind their back. Otherwise, they tend to feel like stabbing you in yours.

A key stakeholder is the customer. Whether you are approaching this project as an internal or external project manager, you should approach the organization for whom you are doing the work as the *customer* or *client*. We use the terms *customer* and *client* interchangeably. Use whichever term works best in your environment, but just make sure you don't confuse the customer or client to whom you and the project team report with the end users of the products of your project, who may also be referred to as customers in some organizations. Both types of customers are important in different ways and at different times. This mindset should help you clarify and prioritize the various competing desires that will be expressed during the opportunity stage.

Stakeholder Identification and Analysis

As a project manager you are concerned with all of the project stakeholders—that is, the people who have a vested interest, or stake, in the activities and results of your project. Using the example of the Dinner Out (DO) project in chapter 2 for illustration, project stakeholders include the following:

- Sponsors who can commit resources and funding. These may also be the project team's customers. In the DO project, the real sponsors of the project were the marketing and sales managers who had to provide the resources to complete the project, not the human resources and purchasing managers, as the project manager initially believed. The human resources and purchasing managers served merely as the initial customers of the project team. As soon as the project got going, the real project customers and sponsors emerged.

- Advocates who can influence the commitment of resources and funding and who will be involved in or affected by the project implementation. The project team's customers or project contacts may actually be advocates in terms of influence, rather than sponsors, as Joe, our project manager in the DO project, found out. He and the project team also discovered additional potential advocates in the store managers, but these advocates had not been brought into the project early enough to help. Instead, the store managers became roadblocks to the project. Correctly identifying and distinguishing between the sponsors and the advocates is an extremely important way to mitigate risk for the project team.

- Technical or subject matter experts who will help you with development and review project work. In our DO project, the store managers and employees were the primary subject matter experts. The marketing and sales staff also provided subject matter content about new store products.

- Product end users or customers who are the people who will use what you produce. The people who would have used the multimedia training would have been the new DO store employees and their managers.

- Suppliers or subcontractors who will be providing services or supplies to support the project effort. Joe, as the MTSI project manager, subcontracted with Alice, an instructional designer, and Pete, an author/programmer. If MTSI had continued with the project, they would also have used the services of a CD-ROM mastering and duplication service.

- Project team members who come from within or outside of the organization to work on parts or all of the project activities. The primary project team members in the DO project were Joe, Alice, and Pete. They also need help and time from the store managers and the marketing staff. One of the problems they ran into was that these other people were not formally made part of the project team.

Although all stakeholders are important to the success of the project, the critical stakeholders during the opportunity stage are the organizational sponsors and advocates. Why? Because these are the people who will:

- Give your team the most all-encompassing view of the expected project vision and goals.
- Provide resources and staff to the project.
- Be responsible for integrating it and selling it to the rest of the organization and the organization's customers.
- Make decisions about whether to proceed or not at each successive project spiral.
- Ultimately decide if the project results meet the criteria they have established.

Many organizations have found it useful to establish a steering committee or group that is involved in setting the overall direction for the project. For example, Business Reengineering Resources, Inc. (BRRI) helps their clients identify executive sponsors and project champions (or advocates) who work with the project team to establish and sell the desired project results.

Don't forget to seek out input from the end users or product customers at this stage. Give every point of view the opportunity to be presented. Mary calls this, "Inviting all the godmothers to the christening," because customers and end users who are not given opportunities to provide their viewpoints and insights have no commitment to making the project work and, through their lack of support or active resistance, can force the project into a comatose "Sleeping Beauty" state from which there may be no Prince Charming to revive it. We have been startled more than once at the range of differences between the views of the project sponsors and those of the ultimate customers or end users regarding the project goals and outcomes. This creates an obvious risk to the success of the implemented product. It is much better to find out up front that there is a problem before too many resources are committed and used.

It has been our experience, and that of many of the other project managers we talked with, that the more contact and involvement we have with the various stakeholders during the opportunity stage, the more success we have throughout the project life cycle. It is a chance to build support, find out problems, identify potential roadblocks, enlist allies, hear new ideas, and generally case out the various individuals' feeling about the project and its intended goals. The networking and ground-breaking work done here will pay off a hundred times over throughout the rest of the project.

Opportunity Stage Output

The outputs of the scoping spiral vary depending on the project and the amount of existing data and analysis available. How much detail is required and how it can be assembled for this initial scoping analysis also depend upon the organization's experience with projects and levels of change similar to those envisioned for this project.

The result is a precisely defined and scoped project, complete with measurable objectives, defined expected results, and explicit critical success factors. In other words, you and the project sponsors should be able to answer the following questions:

- What are we (is the project) trying to do?
- What do we expect to happen as a result?
- How will we go about getting there?
- How will we know when we get there?

The rest of the information gained through the activities in this stage should help to put a clear ring or line around the scope of this project in relationship to any other project and will identify the key organizational and environmental constraints and risks that might affect the project. If, at the end of your tasks, you can't answer at least these four questions and preferably all of the questions listed in Table 3-2 or you do not have commitment to proceed according to the analysis results, proceed with the project at your own peril.

Our recommended approach to getting organizational ideas, review, and buy-in during the opportunity stage can and should, we believe, be applied to all projects, whether they are small, internal organizational improvement projects or large-scale, cross-organizational impact projects. This approach provides the reality test for all ideas. What's the point of wasting any time on a project, even a small one, if the result is not perceived to actually be helpful for the potential stakeholders? We have heard many complaints from people about having to work on projects that the organization doesn't want and need (or won't use the products of when it's all done). It seems to us that, in those cases, the litmus test of determining the project's real value to the organization was not applied before beginning. We have found this lack of value analysis and buy-in is a sure-fire path to project failure. If you and your team are spending your time on activities and projects that have not been completely or properly analyzed and committed to, you are most likely wasting your time.

Commitment Stage

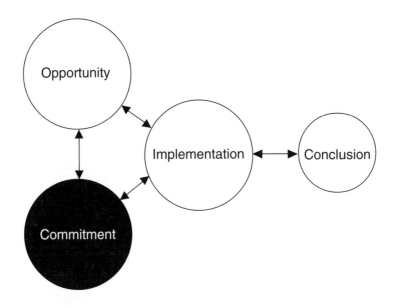

Figure 3-6. Project Management Stages: Commitment

*. . . The best laid plans of mice and men
gang aft aglay.*

—Robert Burns

Table 3-4. Questions to Resolve: Commitment Stage

✔	Questions
	1. Who needs to be involved?
	2. What are the ground rules?
	3. What will we produce and when?
	4. What resources do we need?
	5. What technology will we use to work together?

The main thrust of activities during the commitment stage of the project is to get the right people involved and establish the framework in which they will work. Table 3-4 lists the primary questions that must be resolved in this stage before implementation activities can begin. This part of the project often happens simultaneously with the opportunity stage or is modified and affected by activities that take place during that stage. The commitment stage is also affected by the activities in the implementation stage, particularly as each spiral of implementation activities is completed. During this stage, the project manager must create, out of what seems to be thin air, estimates of how many resources are needed throughout a project life cycle that may last anywhere from a few weeks to several years. This conjuring act is not quite as magical as it seems, although most project managers will tell you that creating the estimates is more art than craft. In this section we will try to demystify some of the conjuring act, while at the same time, alert you to the areas of uncertainty and risk that you should look out for.

Commitment Stage Tasks and Activities

Table 3-5. Commitment Stage Tasks and Activities

✔	Tasks
	1. Define the roles, skills, knowledge, and abilities needed in the project during all of the project spirals.
	2. Determine how to obtain project staff resources (internal and external).
	3. Obtain necessary project staff resources (internal and external).
	4. Establish work rules of operation.
	5. Establish project milestones and schedule.
	6. Determine other resource needs (internal and external).
	7. Obtain necessary project supplies, tools, and technology
	8. Conduct any necessary project staff training.

Table 3-5 lists the fairly straightforward tasks and activities involved in the commitment stage of a project. What's tricky, however, is the development of all of the relevant and related assumptions. One of the first things that needs to be done is to decide how the project can be tackled by asking such questions as:

- Can the project be done by one team of people, or will it require multiple teams?
- Can it be done all at the same time, or will it need to be done over a period of time?
- Do the same people need to be involved at all stages, or will different kinds of people be needed a different times?
- Where are the people we need for this project?
- How will they be able to work with each other?
- Do they need to be in the same place, or can they work in different locations?
- What products does the project need to produce?
- Can the project products be divided up among different teams, or does everyone on the project need to be involved in their production?
- Is there a logical way to group what needs to be done to produce these products, or is that unknowable until you get further into the project?
- What other resources are we going to need to complete the project?
- Do we have ready access to these resources, or is a special effort needed to secure them?

You can see that decisions made here can have an enormous effect on the outcome of any project. One of the primary risks at this stage of a project is the lack of knowledge, or uncertainty, about the answers to these kinds of questions. Such uncertainty can lead to incorrect decisions—decisions that will jeopardize your ability to complete the project within the time and cost estimates you make at this stage of the project. "On time and within budget" is the chant uttered by all project managers and their sponsors when asked about their criteria for a successful project. The problem with this criteria is that the schedule dates and budget numbers lack validity at later stages of the project. As more project activities are completed, and more changes occur in your knowledge and understanding of the project goals and objectives and of the possible ways of producing the correct solution, the more likely it is that the assumptions you made early on are incorrect, and incomplete. This often puts you in the position of trying to explain why you can't meet or achieve your own project plan. Although we cannot solve this problem completely, we can offer you some strategies for minimizing the shock of "not meeting plan" before it happens. The next sections in this chapter look at some of the major questions and issues you should think about when constructing your plans BEFORE you commit yourself and your team to an impossible dream.

Who Needs to Be Involved?

The identification of the project team and all other project stakeholders is begun in the opportunity stage, as soon as the project idea is formed and assigned (or initiated). You should begin the commitment stage by identifying all the roles and responsibilities that need to be performed to complete the project. Then, you should identify who might best be able to perform those roles. Then you need to determine whether you have those kind of people available to you, and if so how you can get them involved in or assigned to the project. This may require some juggling to get the right people who have the right skills, knowledge, and experience, particularly if the project involves something in which your organization has little experience or knowledge.

A former project of Lori's serves as a good example. An insurance company that needed a new financial management and accounting system to better track its income and expenses decided that it did not have the in-house expertise in its information systems department to design and develop this kind of system. In addition, no one there had much experience in managing a large-scale software development project. Management decided the best approach to solving these resource problems was to buy the solution, in this case by hiring a large accounting company's consulting services to manage the project and provide the necessary software designers and programmers. The insurance company's own accounting and programming staff was used as project team members to work alongside the outside contractors, learning as the project went along so that they could take over implementation of the system once it was completed and installed.

Whether for internal or external staff, it is important to develop a set of roles and responsibilities that can be used to secure staff and clarify its duties while involved in the project. These roles and responsibilities can and should be refined by the project team as people get involved in the project and begin to figure out what needs to be done.

Many times the decision whether to use internal resources or buy outside resources is solely based on money or time, as in, "We don't have the money in our budget to pay for outside contractors," or "We don't have the time to train our staff to be competent to do this project." We suggest that you do not forget to factor in the other important elements in this decision. The resource roles and responsibilities lists created during the commitment stage contain the elements that must take place to make the project work, and many times these roles cannot be performed by anyone other than the designated internal resource. You need to consider the long-term project goals when making any resource requests and decisions.

One of the problems we and other project managers have had with getting internal resources is that once the project team is assigned and specific dates for project work determined, there is a great deal of resistance to changing either the people or the times allotted for participating. It's one of the classic Catch-22 situations—if you are honest about the extent of time and expertise required, your request is sometimes refused because it seems like too much. However, if you underestimate the time and expertise required to get the project started, you need to beg later for additional appropriate resources. Both positions are risky, with little opportunity to recover from a bad decision.

The project manager will also have to decide the best strategy for getting the right people involved in the project. Whether through cajolery, bribery, borrowing, purchase, or lease, obtaining the right project resources is critical. If you don't have the people with the right expertise and organizational knowledge and clout, your time and cost estimates will have even less probability of being accurate. The wrong people might mean that you will have to spend precious time training the project staff to do things for which you could have contracted directly. Or it might mean that some team members try to do things they really don't know how to do, and make critical mistakes. Or it might mean that because of a lack of the right organizational knowledge your team develops something that doesn't meet the end-user organization's needs. All the possible scenarios are so filled with uncertainty, that it is a guaranteed certainty that something wrong will happen. Reduce your risk by spending the time and money to get the right people involved from the start.

For example, if you know that your product will be marketed to retailers in several countries, hire consultants who are knowledgeable about the customs, culture, and languages of those countries. Have them review your graphics and written information to ensure that your materials will translate well into other environments and that your publications will be as attractive when converted into another language. In another example, if you are an internal project manager, get your human resources organization and staff involved in any project that will result in major changes in work processes. They can help you build the new human resource system that will be needed to support the new work processes, such as new position descriptions and new skills training. Without those kind of institutional commitments, your new and improved system will fail.

What Are the Ground Rules?

The ground rules for each project vary depending upon the organization in which the project is taking place and the type of project that is being done. Ground rules should include operating assumptions and rules of operations covering both work processes issues and content issues. You can mitigate a lot of risk by setting up these ground rules early. You should also establish a process for modifying these ground rules as the project continues through its life cycle as you and the project team learn more about the project and the process and discover better ways of doing things. Some of the kinds of ground rules we have had to establish for our projects are discussed in the following sections.

Set Out and Define Turf Boundaries. These include boundaries between design teams versus operating teams, marketing departments versus production departments versus human resources departments, and so on. Boundaries can delineate either content or work processes. This is the first test of the roles and responsibilities you set up earlier. Take the time to clarify these boundaries early, otherwise you will spend countless hours later trying to clear up misunderstandings and stave off duplicate work. Setting up these roles and boundaries can be a difficult task, especially if the project involves something new to the organization. Be prepared to refine these as the project continues and the teams learn more about what is really required. Define roles of the stakeholder groups that are not actively involved in the project team, as well. These other groups, such as external project customers or executive sponsors or other organizational advocates, may not be involved in the day-to-day workings of the project but will be involved at some other stages of the project and you need to see that they are included in the overall plan.

One of the decisions you will be making along with the turf boundary decisions is whether or not to split up the project work among different teams. This is, of course, a situational question, depending upon where you are in the project life cycle and whether or not the work can be divided neatly. We have found that early project stage work is better done with one cross-functional team for as long as possible. This ensures that everyone on the team is involved in the gathering, analyzing, and synthesizing of the initial information required for decision making throughout the rest of the project. When the project begins working on specific, specialized development tasks, the project team may be divided and added to with more experts to assist in the work.

A word of caution, however. Maintaining an integrated working group (i.e., a group that represents more than one stakeholder or specialty point of view) or specialized work action (SWAT) team is critical in minimizing risk on an ongoing basis. The major failures that we have read or heard about or seen with our own eyes have occurred because one stakeholder group working on a project made a decision without input from the other groups, causing all sorts of negative fallout in the rest of the project. So, to prevent that from happening to you, we strongly recommend that even if you divide up into smaller work teams, you keep the staffing on those teams cross-organizational and cross-specialty.

Division of the work is another tricky issue. If you divide up the work as on an assembly line, you build in critical dependencies that could jeopardize the project timelines, especially when the expected unexpected event happens early in a project, altering a planned task upstream from other planned tasks. A way we have found to minimize this risk is to divide and assign work in chunks (this is a technical term we use!) that are big enough to be thought of as interim or partial products. This is akin to what some auto manufacturers have discovered works better in building cars. Final assembly of cars is now done by teams who can integrate their work to create the actual project, on the spot, instead of handing off portions of the work to each other. Applying this principle to smaller projects, Lori has divided up work on performance support projects along content lines (e.g., all customer service materials versus all accounting materials) instead of by type of output (on-line help versus print or on-line reference versus on- or off-line tutorials). That way her subteams can integrate their efforts, reducing redundancies and overlap. Plus, this gives the subteams the added incentive of ownership of a product, something she likes (and has found helps) to motivate her and her teams.

Establish Communication Strategies. Communication links between teams and with other stakeholders must be determined. You need to avoid setting up artificial networks or boundaries between people who need to communicate. Make sure that everyone gets the information they need. We have found that more information is always better than less, so tend to build strategies that allow for a continuous feedback loop between all project stakeholders, both inside the project team and outside. This is related to the turf/boundary ground rules, because providing and using information to and from all of the project teams is part of the decision making about how and when you need to split up the work. Be careful to make sure the flow of necessary information to all project participants is assured in your communication system.

One example of where this didn't happen was in the case of the NASA shuttle Challenger accident. Investigators looking into the January 1988 explosion following liftoff of the Challenger were told that the Rockwell engineers had, in fact, expressed concerns to their local management about the advisability of scheduling a liftoff in the cold conditions that existed that week. Those concerns were not communicated to management at the Flight Control Center, who authorized the liftoff. The tragic result might have been averted if the right information had been available to those making the liftoff decision (Vaughn 1996).

Establish Work Procedures and Guidelines. This includes determining policies regarding organizational approaches, process expectations, reporting and documentation requirements, output quality and format criteria, and issue resolution processes. Laying out as many of the expectations as possible reduces the chances that someone will do something later in the project that will threaten its completion. Some of these guidelines may need to be established prior to assembling the team, but we have found that involving the team in defining and refining these guidelines is a good way to make sure everyone knows what is required and how it should be done. It also provides a way to get the team members to buy in to the project and its process approach.

We have established project guidelines for such matters as: work environment (on-site or off-site), work attire (business dress, business casual, shorts or sweats, jammies), group process (all input is valued, one conversation at a time), work hours (fixed, floating, core hours by time zone), reporting and feedback (in writing, via e-mail, on electronic bulletin board or listserve), document processing (software used, file transfer procedures, communications protocols), product output criteria (electronic or print, draft or edited, depth of treatment), and format and quality criteria (looks, style, layout). We also try to lay out a working approach to the project, what overall assumptions we are operating under, how people are expected to participate and when, when different people in different roles have greater or lesser input into decision making, how to handle issues and concerns that come up, and how to provide feedback to one another and others outside of the project team.

Establish Review Process and Criteria. Early in the project the initial teams need to establish critical success factors for the project and the measures to be used to assess accomplishment of the specific project objectives and critical success factors. How those measures will then be evaluated is part of what needs to be described in any overall project review process. This process should outline who does what kind of review, when that review will take place, how the review will be conducted, what standards or criteria will be used by the reviewers, and what effect or impact the review will have on the progress of the project. Some of the criteria, such as specific product format or style criteria, may need to be developed at a later stage of the project. For example, in software development projects, specific screen design format criteria are usually not possible in early implementation spirals. However, general criteria can be established (e.g., integrates with currently used organizationwide system interface) as well as parameters for more specific criteria that will be established later (e.g., all system screens will meet human factors guidelines for user interface).

Because the review process is so closely tied to decisions about how to proceed with the project, this is a very critical issue in risk management. Determining what reviewers are looking at and how they should be making decisions is the important task here. More than once we have discovered that reviewers could (and may have) stop(ed) a project based on their assessments of elements of the project deliverables that were not even considered in the original product specifications. We recognize that new factors will come into play in later stages and deliverables of a project, that is, the certain uncertainty we have learned to expect. One thing we suggest you do to manage this is to reassess the review criteria before each project deliverable review. Make sure the list of criteria is still complete and accurate. If not, modify it to encompass current issues that should be included in the review.

Another way to nminimize the risk of a review that is so negative that it stops or delays the project is to make sure that what the reviewers are examining reflects a complete picture of the desired project output. In multimedia development projects, for example, Tim Spannaus and Collette Pariseau of Emdicium, Inc., require that all reviews be done using actual prototypes of the desired finished product, rather than on storyboards that simply describe what is supposed to be shown, said, or interacted with. They have discovered, as have many others of us involved in systems development projects, that how things look and feel on a system screen (i.e., a prototype) is very different to a user or reviewer than how it looks and feels on a printed page (i.e., a storyboard). Changes made based on reviews of storyboards too often have required duplicate work be done and redone after later system testing and user reviews of the prototype. You can easily avoid such extra or redundant work by reviewing prototypes instead!

Identify Risk Assessment Factors. This should include projectwide and product-specific factors. Part of the underlying theme of all the ground rule and operating procedures you establish should be the questions, What should we do if this doesn't work? and How will we know it isn't working? Having the project team help you identify the possible risk items that will trigger problems with the project is a good way to encourage the notion that all project team members should be actively involved in risk management. Problems are always easier to solve if found early enough to take corrective action. Identify the potential trouble areas early, then watch out for symptoms. Part of risk management is reducing the stress of the surprise problem. If you've prepared yourself for most of the possible problems, you are more likely to be calm when the unexpected problem occurs. You can save the energy you would have used being upset for exploring solutions. Although this approach and frame of mind hasn't eliminated all our venting and whining, it has reduced it a great deal, allowing us to feel better able to manage the various project uncertainties as they come up. Yes, this is primarily a suggestion about attitude, but we can testify that it does work.

What Will We Produce and When?

The answers to the question, What will we produce and when? should include preliminary product output specifications, major deliverable milestones, and proposed due dates for those milestones. Don't try to specify all interim products. Instead, establish with your team clear and regular reassessment points and criteria, or at least, assessment criteria-setting guidelines. This should give you more than enough information and control over the quality and progress of the project. We have found a simple work plan format such as the one shown in Figure 3-7 helps us keep our projects on track.

Activity	Time/Date	Resources	Deliverable	Evaluation/ Use
Identify alternatives to tracking software	Weeks 4-5	Information services, accounts receivable, Station employees project team	Analysis of alternatives, including: the estimated cost of each alternative and recommended alternative	Selection of the most cost-effective, cost-efficient software that meets functional requirements
Identify jobs impacted by change	Week 7	Project team, Human resources	Schedule of positions potentially impacted by change	To be used by human resources identifying job descriptions to be rewritten

Figure 3-7. Sample Work Plan Format with Content Examples

We also like to make sure that we track all categories of relevant work activity. Categories or groups of activities that can be included in most project plans include:

- **Organizational mission links, project goals, objectives, and critical success factors.** Typical activities include:
  — Establish organizational mission and project objective links.
  — Develop project vision and goals.
  — Develop organizational resources and support for project.
  — Develop policies for resulting work processes, output, and results.
  — Establish project critical success factors and measures.
- **Work process and product design and development.** Typical activities include:
  — Establish project goals and criteria.
  — Conduct work function and task requirements analysis.
  — Establish technology application feasibility.
  — Develop data or other requirements for new technology.
  — Develop procedures and standards for new work process, tasks, and products.
- **Technology.** Typical activities include:
  — Develop requirements for and procure and install system hardware and software.
  — Design, develop, and test system and application software.
  — Prepare a plan to design, develop, and distribute system software and hardware documentation.
  — Determine maintenance and support requirements.
  — Prototype, test, and field test system.
  — Evaluate system.
- **Support systems.** Typical activities include:
  — Determine requirements.
  — Develop recruitment and selection procedures.

- Review and propose appropriate personnel practices.
- Determine requirements for and establish communications systems.
- Determine and establish support and maintenance procedures and resources.

- **Human resource competence.** Typical activities include:
  - Determine new and changed training needs.
  - Design and develop training systems and procedures.
  - Delineate staff roles and locations where they will be carried out (training, management, users, system development, and system support).
  - Develop or procure user (and system support) training.
  - Evaluate training system and programs.

- **Financial resources.** Typical activities include:
  - Analyze cost feasibility.
  - Track project expense and resource use.
  - Complete regular budget status and activity reports.
  - Assure continuous funding throughout life of project.

- **Physical resources.** Typical activities include:
  - Determine requirements.
  - Select and prepare sites.
  - Procure and distribute furniture and supplies.
  - Plan life cycle physical support.

- **Project management and administration.** Typical activities include:
  - Integrate resources and activities throughout project.
  - Measure and evaluate project outputs, results, and savings.
  - Develop and monitor communications and issues resolution plans.

- **Public relations/change agentry and management.** Typical activities include:
  - Provide regular internal and external communications and notifications.
  - Develop and present project review and announcement briefings.

— Design, develop, and perform other activities to coordinate and communicate project tasks and accomplishments.

These categories represent the types of concerns and issues that should be addressed in any project that is making any substantial change to the work or output of an organization. They also represent the systems view and quantum view that we take in any project: that any change in one part of the system affects all other parts of the system. You will find, as we have, that by taking this global, whole-systems approach to your work, you will reduce significantly the amount of risk you encounter throughout your projects. Thinking about the organizational interactions, and their accompanying uncertainty, helps you plan and account for some of the issues that will arise. It won't help you discover all of them; you'll create some uncertainties in your own interactions, too. However, this systems approach should keep you from unwittingly creating unnecessary uncertainties and risks. Most times, that's all the edge we have as project managers. We encourage you to search out the possible alligators before beginning your journey through the swamp, so you are better armed to defend yourself and your project stakeholders as you work to make it through successfully to the dry land beyond.

Setting Timelines and Output Specifications

You can have it fast, cheap, or good, but only two out of the three at the same time.

—Anonymous, but much cited

We have found one of the quickest ways to slow down a project and stifle design creativity is to set tight timelines and detailed output requirements. "Huh?" you say. "I thought tight timelines and specific output requirements would speed up a project and keep it on track."

Well, so did we in our earlier lives as project managers. We've learned the hard way that you can't command people to think and create in preconceived boxes and in designated time-frames. Oh yes, they can produce mountains of reports and lines and lines of code in incredibly short periods of time, but that doesn't mean that what they produce is useful or even appropriate for the problem or situation at hand.

What seems to work better for most people—that is, what gets more creative and quicker results—is a more fluid approach to timelines and outputs. We suggest that you emulate Timm Esque, project manager for Intel Corporation's business practices network, who has found that setting deadlines for short-term results only is the most effective approach. Commit resources to each mini-project, or interim deliverable (e.g., each project prototype), then rebudget for the remaining project products based on the results of that mini-project, as you know more about what is really needed next.

Do specify what decisions need to be made to proceed with the project. You may also want to specify how the information should be presented so that you can make the right decisions. This is related to our discussion earlier about reviews using prototypes. We have found that bad decisions are made when the decision makers have incomplete information or information in the wrong format. Help people make the right decisions.

For example, in the multimedia development project described in chapter 2, the first interim deliverable might be the design vision or concept agreement memo, which describes the intent, look, and feel of the vision. This would describe the content to be included, the instructional strategies and media to be used, and the work situations to be demonstrated. The second interim deliverable could be an initial prototype of the design vision to prove the concept and make sure this is really what is wanted (e.g., a sample lesson complete with graphics and test questions). The third interim deliverable would be the final prototype, which adds any modifications made based on the review and testing of the first prototype and pushes the prototype a bit further toward the vision. This would probably be a complete lesson and the overall CD-ROM interface. Upon approval of this deliverable the design is frozen and taken into production.

"Wait a minute," you say. "Where is the requirements document, the technical blueprint, the target user analysis, the detailed design document, the storyboards, and so on?" The answer is you might still develop and use them, but they might not be the critical outputs that will help you and your client make the ultimate decisions about whether this approach solves the stated problem or achieves the stated goal. Don't make the mistake of defining *deliverables* as the various pieces of paper that are typically produced throughout a project. This has the unfortunate effect of keeping the project team focused on creating those outputs, rather than the project results sought.

Concentrate on solving the original problem and reaching your goal by producing the desired end product, and you can eliminate some of the time-consuming paperwork that only documents *effort*, not *results*. By continually driving toward producing successive replicas or prototypes of the desired end product, you can actually see whether or not the idea works, rather than just speculate about it.

Documentation, Creativity, and Schedules

Another advantage to focusing on the design vision rather than on project documentation is that it allows you to concentrate on the most important part of the project, rather than be distracted and sidetracked into producing lengthy reports that drain time and enthusiasm. Does this mean you shouldn't require documentation? Not at all. In fact, documentation is one of the main ways you can mitigate risk. In a *Multimedia Producer* article, Kathy Kozel describes how the Virgin Sound & Vision in-house multimedia development group commits itself to updating all design and production documents within 24 hours of all changes, even small ones (1996, 100). Says their producer, "Entropy happens. Things get out of control so fast. Keeping documents up is a lot of work, but it's the only way."

What this means is that the kind and format of the documentation, particularly for analysis and design work, are often better defined during or after the creative work is done. Let your team set any necessary specific interim output requirements they need to proceed with the work at hand. You make sure you and your organization get enough information to make the critical go/no go decisions at each spiral of the project implementation.

"How will I know we're still going in the right path and are getting it done in time?" you ask. We're tempted to say, "Trust us. It'll be okay." What we will say instead is, "Trust your teams." If you've jointly established the goals and vision for the project and gotten commitment from the people involved in creating the vision, they and you will be able to figure out what has to be done and when it isn't getting done. It is just that the same standard set of reports will not work for every project. Decision points and outputs will differ. Think decision points—what we really need to see or hear to make the right decision about proceeding? Ask for that, then get out of the way. Pounds of paper will not save you if you end up with a failed project. Detailed time reports showing time spent on writing those reports won't tell you if you are still on schedule. Besides, if you already know all the answers, why do you need to do the project, anyway?

Accountability and Project Planning

Timm Esque of Intel Corporation described their approach to project planning, which they call accomplishment-based project planning (Esque 1996). They have used this approach successfully with 100 projects. He says this collaborative decision making has resulted in realistic budget and time estimates.

At the start of a project, the project manager develops a requirements list and schedules a full-day meeting with all stakeholders—project staff and client—to agree on expectations and to set criteria for how project outcomes will be measured. In this meeting, they identify all customers and reach agreement on what will be delivered and on who will do what, by when, and how well. Then, using Post-its®, the people present at the meeting place their names on the deliverables for which they agree to be responsible. The project manager asks for a commitment for a short term (e.g., eight weeks) and then develops a plan and budget based on these commitments that are presented to management (or as we call them, the sponsors). Although management has often resisted the estimates developed by the stakeholder meeting, the plans developed in these meetings have resulted in high-quality deliverables, produced without overtime and with the cooperation of workers, customers, and managers.

As Esque says in a *Performance Improvement* article (October 1996, 32), "Participants in accomplishment-based project planning leave their events with a high-level plan for their project that identifies who will deliver what to whom and when. While the participants create their project plan, they share their assumptions with each other about how they will evaluate the quality of certain deliverables that will be passed from one functional group to another." In this project management model, all stakeholders are aware of how decisions were made and all accept the outcomes of their joint thinking.

We think this is a terrific idea to mitigate the risks of flawed project estimates. This, or some variation of it, should help you stay on track and give you enough flexibility to make changes in the plan when you need to.

Rob Foshay at TRO Learning, Inc. (1996), recommends a similar approach based on his experience as the manager of quality assurance and standards. He says that the most difficult aspect of managing a project is determining the right balance among time, task, and resources. He has found, particularly in organizations that don't have very much experience in doing these kinds of project estimates, that the expectations rarely match the reality. They often want, and expect, fixed time estimates tied to fixed budgets, when the reality of the project demands shorter-term estimates, with future work being determined based on initial results. This uncertainty drives some organizations crazy, but ignoring it doesn't make it go away. Organizations that insist on a fixed-time, fixed-budget project often find they end up having to pay for additional projects to fix what didn't work from the initial project. Or they merely settle for an inadequate solution to the problem that triggered the project. Avoid these risks. Help educate your clients and customers so they know that it almost always costs less to do it right—that is, incrementally and completely—rather than hurrying up to get as much done as can be finished by some arbitrary deadline or fixed dollar amount.

Money, Time, and People Resources

Resources come in many flavors. The primary project resources that you need to deal with are money, time, and people. We've talked a bit earlier in this section about time and people. Money is a different story entirely, although it is related to some of the people, specifically the sponsors, who are the funding sources for your project. Much has been written about the care and feeding of project sponsors. We especially subscribe to some of the advice and recommendations from Daryl Conner in the *Managing at the Speed of Change* (1995) and Kathy Farrell and Craig Broude in *Winning the Change Game* (1987). Conner particularly emphasizes the need to keep the sponsor involved and invested in the success of the project to ensure continued funding. He offers the following advice to those of us serving as project managers and change agents:

"Don't work harder than your sponsor. You should never mask poor sponsorship by acting as a pseudo-sponsor when the person or group who should be playing that role falters in their duties. When your sponsor cannot or will not take the proper steps to legitimize the change and reinforce the targets, it should be taken as a sign that the project is no longer of sufficient importance to proceed. Let the sponsor know this so that he or she can either adjust priorities or formally delay or terminate the project."

This is clear advice to keep focused on the sponsor, rather than be diverted with trying to drum up support among the advocates of the project. Remember that advocates are the people who cannot directly authorize money for the project. They can be seen as helpers in convincing and reminding the sponsor about how important the project is, but the ultimate person to be sold is the sponsor. Don't ever forget that in managing your project's budget and funding. We have heard countless tales from project managers about lost funding, the logical risk of failing to follow this advice. Most of the evidence you need to initially sell the project will be gained through the activities in the opportunity stage. However, in developing your plans for the rest of the project, as you are doing now in the commitment stage, be sure to build in a line item that includes activities that support continued involvement and funding support from the sponsor. What those activities are depends upon the kind and size of your organization and the kinds of funding mechanisms that are available to you. Just don't forget to do them.

For example, include in your project timeline frequent briefings and status reports, so your sponsor is never in doubt about what the project is doing, or the progress to date. And of course, your customer should always be informed of and agree to any significant change to project timelines or deliverables, especially if they are value-added changes that shorten cycles to complete work more quickly, for example, or improve the quality of deliverables by incorporating new data.

A related area of concern is to make sure to provide for continuous funding throughout the project. Because you don't want suppliers and subcontractors to stop work on the project due to lack of payment, you must provide a way to get continuous payment to the project. Some projects set up regular payment schedules based on the calendar (e.g., every two weeks, every month). Other projects tie payments to deliverables. If the latter is the approach you use, another factor you should consider in developing your project deliverables schedule is how you need to cover your project financially. This then adds another risk that you will have to manage, the effect of delays in scheduled deliveries on the project cash flow. In the building trade, a standard billing practice is to have the client pay for the materials up front and then pay monthly invoices for the labor expended. This reduces the contractor's risk for being left with the bill for materials if any disputes arise during the project. It also provides regular checkpoints for examining progress and determining if any changes need to be made before going forward, thereby reducing the risk that the project will not meet the goals.

The project manager must balance the client's ability to pay on a schedule with the client's need to see results before payment and with your need to keep your deliverable schedule as results oriented as possible. These seem like mutually exclusive issues, but can be managed if you think about them in relationship with one another while you are developing your project plans. The best way to do this is to develop trust by establishing a collaborative relationship from the project outset. Make sure that you provide an early prototype and present it in a face-to-face meeting with the customer, so that the customer takes ownership of the project and develops confidence that you are eager to have customer input and determined to provide high-quality, high-value products or services. This kind of relationship can allow you to easily and honestly discuss requirements changes with the customer as they come up during these review sessions. Michael Hillelsohn, an experienced project manager with The Orkand Corporation, cautions us to not let that "good relationship itself . . . lead to requirements creep where the changes are small and subtle, and the developer, who is eager to please the customer, says yes too often. The response usually should be, yes and these are the risks and cost and schedule implications of doing that (1996, 27).

Resources Other Than Money, Time, and People

You will need to plan for obtaining, or making available, other specific resources that will be needed by the project teams to complete their work; for example:

- Technology (this resource is discussed in detail later in this section).
- Space or facilities.
- Furniture.
- Equipment.

- Supplies (e.g., paper, pens, tape, building materials).
- Services (e.g., delivery, copying).

This seems like an easy set of activities, that can be handled by any good administrative assistant. Why are we mentioning them in a book for project managers? Because not attending to these requirements and potentially choosing the wrong type or supplier of the required resource can lead to risks throughout the rest of the project. And because these decisions reflect selections and requirements that may be needed to implement the final project solution, the wrong choices can jeopardize the project's success. Those of us managing far-flung project teams have learned the hard way that these issues can make or break the effective functioning of a project team.

Don't dismiss this area as unimportant in setting up your project. One example of how a bad decision about providing resources led to the near failure of a project was in a project to develop a training curriculum plan for customer service representatives in a telecommunications company. The external contractor project manager agreed to the client's demand that a project team member, a subcontractor, work on-site. Several problems arose. The client did not have the workspace set up when the contract started, so several days were lost while the internal contact and the contractor tried to get the necessary technology and supplies available. Then, the technology provided did not include the correct version of software for the project deliverable being created, so work that was done on-site had to be translated into the correct software at the contractor's site, causing duplicate work. A big time waster on-site were the conversations and interruptions that occurred when office members dropped by to chat with the subcontractor. Another major problem was the client's project manager's habit of asking the subcontractor to participate in staff meetings, many of which did not directly concern the project. By the time the major project deliverable was due, the subcontractor had to construct it in about half the time that had been originally budgeted in order to meet the deadline, which the client would not change. The quality of the deliverable was compromised leading to unpleasant arguments over the quality and completeness of the deliverable. The project could not be counted as a success, but we did learn yet another risk to consider in project resource management.

There is no absolute answer to any of the issues involved in securing and providing project resources. We have more stories than we have space to tell about the problems involved in trying to resolve software version discrepancies or in providing copies of product deliverables to the client in the right form. We've gradually learned to deal with these problems by making sure that we get very detailed in this part of our plan, establishing specific requirements for how things will be done, delivered, and paid for. If you don't figure out these issues, you risk not meeting your project deliverables schedule and budget. Work these items out early to avoid the continual aggravation they will give you if you don't.

For example, if your project is developing software documentation, you need to reach agreement with the customer on who is responsible for alerting your project staff to changes. However, this will not guarantee that you will be kept informed of ongoing modifications. Creative programmers, working long hours under tight timeframes, seldom take the initiative to communicate with the project people responsible for documentation. In our experience, the documentation can only be kept current with the software versions if the project manager and the team establish excellent rapport with the software writing team, and a project staff member is assigned to visit the programmers' site frequently and thus capture changes as they are being made and act as a reminder that the documentation team needs their help.

The Technology Resource

One of the major resources that must be obtained is the technology needed to develop the project products and facilitate the project's process. Those of you in large organizations that supply office workspaces complete with all necessary equipment and technology may forget this step, assuming the use of existing stuff (another technical term). Others of you who work in less-well-equipped organizations, or in free-standing consulting environments, know only too well that nothing can be assumed to be in place and operating. No matter on which end of the range you sit, we suggest you include this task on your project management checklist.

Each kind of project demands different kinds of technology. The kind and location of staff resources and other stakeholders also influences what technology is needed for your project. We recommend that you determine the project technology requirements for the following areas of project activities:

- Communication between and within teams.
- Communication with clients and other stakeholders.
- Cost and schedule management.
- Product and process documentation.
- Design and prototyping tools.
- Output development tools.

Few projects (at least the ones we've been involved in) exist in a vacuum. Most are situated within an environment with certain types of technology in place, such as computers and workstations, standard office automation software, existing e-mail and voice mail systems, telephones, and fax machines. What is less standard are file transfer and posting capabilities; external communications links or services; computer-assisted software engineering (CASE) tools; documentation systems; design, prototyping, and development tools; and project management scheduling and cost-tracking systems. Many of these nonstandard technologies are nonstandard because of their specialized uses and specialized work environments. However, we have found that we can share tools with our clients to help make us all more productive during the project. One of our overriding principles in determining how we are going to produce products is to try to avoid doing anything twice. That usually means trying to use the technology that is going to be used in the end product or using the same technology as the client organization so that the final product can be modified and reused after the project is completed.

To select the right technology you and the project team should:

- Determine specific project requirements according to activities and user involvement.
- Assess quality and appropriateness of existing tools for all requirements.
- Analyze necessity and cost for additional technical resources.
- Secure appropriate technological tools for all project users and project products.

The risks here are obvious—choosing the wrong technology for either the project process or the project product or solution, or both. We have had experience with all of these options, as, we are sure, have all of you. Is there a way to mitigate the risk? The only way we have found is to keep focused on the project results or goals and choose technology that helps lead you toward them. You can be diverted into trying out all sorts of tools and programs that are sold to you as the answer. We're here to tell you that none of them is the perfect answer. All require time and effort to use and implement. You need to balance potential return with the actual investment of effort. Information systems departments are still having a hard time realizing some of the promised productivity gains from their new systems. Part of that problem is due to the lack of definition and collection of data on the achievement measures, but the rest of that problem is a simple underestimation in the amount of effort (time, resources, in-depth learning) required to institute the use of new technologies. Don't make the same mistake in trying to determine the best technology to use in your project. If you need to move to a new technology, and many times you will, build in the appropriate time and activities to implement them effectively. This investment will more than pay for itself, in terms of project productivity. You can also get added benefits if you are using a new technology that will eventually be used as part of the project solution. The experience your project team and stakeholders get through the use of this technology will jump-start the installation and implementation process of that solution.

Two examples illustrate this, one involving hard technology, the other using soft technology. In the hard technology example, a project team was working on developing more effective and efficient ways to conduct meetings and exchange information for an international organization with many global affiliates. They explored the use of video teleconferencing technologies, Intranet and Internet communications technologies, and computer conferencing software. One of the first ways they tested the viability of these technologies was to use them in their project work among the team members who were scattered around the globe. The lessons they learned in trying to conduct their project work were instantly built into their project prototypes for wider-scale testing. By the time they were ready to roll out the product solution, they had already worked out many of the obvious bugs in the technology and had built up a large group of interested and experienced users who could help with the next stage of implementation. This is the "hitting two birds with one stone" strategy (or the "twofer" for short), a strategy we heartily endorse and recommend and obviously another way to mitigate risk.

The soft technology example involves modeling new behaviors in project work that reflect desired organizational behavior at project completion. This strategy is used in most successful reengineering, total quality management, and other human performance improvement projects. The technologies are soft in that they don't involve hardware, software, or mechanical tools, but instead involve organizational and individual behavior technologies or ways of doing things. However, the principle is exactly the same. Use these technologies while working on the project to introduce them and get the stakeholders used to them and experienced in them so that the project stakeholders become the advocates and implementers of the solution when it is delivered or implemented in the organization. This is how you can build in long-term success. In their reengineering projects, Business Reengineering Resources, Inc. (BRRI), teaches and demonstrates the new behaviors that the redesigned organization will need, things such as respectful communications, small group work, team decision making, cooperative goal setting, and process maintenance. They also establish the project working environment to allow the project participants to get used to working in the kind of environment that will be established in the redesigned organization. Then they help the participants get used to behaving appropriately throughout the project. The project team, which by design includes representatives of all of the major stakeholder groups, becomes the new organization by the time the project work is completed. They know it can work because it did for them. Talk about reducing anxiety and risk!

Risk Management, Proposals, and Commitments

We've talked throughout this section about the various risks that can arise during the commitment stage. Most of the risks are caused by the uncertainties implicit in your assumptions in creating your project plans. If you guess wrong on any one of the items in which you are trying to get commitment, you endanger the ability of the project team to complete the project.

The General Accounting Office (GAO), the U.S. government agency that audits other government departments and programs for Congress, has done extensive work on analyzing and mitigating risk during proposal development (Cowie 1996). In response to pressure to reduce costs and time to complete projects, the GAO has developed a series of risk assessment questions and has integrated them into a job model.

Here are some of the questions the GAO uses to assesses the risk in a new project (you can adapt this list to the parameters of your own project to review your own plans and commitments):

- Is the cost of the project over $500,000? Usually there is a relationship among cost, size, and complexity of the effort required, size and types of staff needed, project duration, and managerial challenge involved. (You may use a lower figure, but this relationship will be relevant in any project.)
- Does the project involve a sensitive or controversial subject? If so, the products will receive closer scrutiny, which may result in extensive and slow reviews—and potentially in costly revisions.
- Will a complex methodology be required? The more complex the methodology, the greater the need for time-consuming and costly arrangements and sophisticated analyses.
- Is there likely to be disagreement about the final deliverables? Sometimes different stakeholders look at the product outcomes from different perspectives. An outcome that satisfies one may not satisfy another.

- Can the due date to complete the project be met, given the scope and the methodology required? Although you should not be a prisoner of timetables, you will always be working within an overall timeframe within which project activities must be completed and funds expended. In the case of the GAO, the congressional office requesting the audit sets the deadline.
- Will staff with the requisite skills be available when they are needed? What will be the impacts on the project if key staff are unavailable because of leave time, retirements, or commitments to other projects? Are such events as strikes or weather likely to impact project work?
- Can the project be justified from a cost/benefit perspective? If not, you should reconsider taking it on. As a project manager, you need to be able to answer this question in the affirmative, because it can be very costly to you and your client if, when the project is partially completed, the client perceives that the benefits do not justify the cost and cancels the project.

These review questions are a good starting point for you when reviewing your own project plans for areas of risk. We discuss some others in chapter 7.

Commitment Stage Output

Whatever the output of this stage, whether a proposal, design specifications, project implementation plan, letter of commitment, or some combination of these, make sure you assess the risk inherent in your various assumptions and planned activities. Build in activities to reassess these assumptions and plans at appropriate intervals in your project schedule. Remember that you are building these commitments and plans to meet the goals and objectives itemized in the opportunity stage. If, during the creation of your project plans, or during the implementation of the plans, you find that the assumptions change your understanding of those goals, or change some of the original project objectives and critical success factors, we urge you to inform the project stakeholders immediately, so that the project opportunity can be reevaluated.

For example, in one project a member of the project team discovered that paychecks of employees at a key supplier's had been returned for insufficient funds. This totally unexpected evidence that the supplier was in serious financial straits represented a serious threat to the project, since the supplier was contracted to provide a unique software application not available from any other source. The project manager informed her customer at once of this troubling news, and the project returned to the opportunity stage to reevaluate the project goals in light of this unforeseen development. It is all right to return to the opportunity stage—better to get these issues resolved before too many resources are expended.

When there is a fit between the project opportunity goals and the plans and commitments for executing the project, you are ready to begin work. You mean this wasn't work? you ask in dismay. You're right. It was and is work to define the opportunity and clarify the plans and commitments necessary to get the project off the ground. The risk we have found here is that you and your client don't recognize the need to do this work before beginning the actual project work or to do it in such a way as to reduce the possibility of successful project outcomes. Nearly every one of the problems we have run into during project implementation has had its roots in the assumptions and plans made here, in the commitment stage, or in the incomplete analyses done during the opportunity stage. Make sure that you don't set yourself up to fail before you even start your project.

Implementation Stage

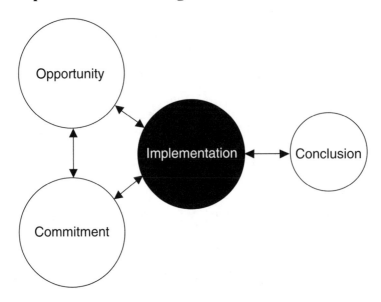

Figure 3-8. Project Management Stages: Implementation

Implementation . . . it's about time! Implementation, as we are using the term, covers a wide range and type of tasks, depending upon the kind of project you are managing. Full development projects, like those to build a building, an airplane, a new manufacturing plant device, an information system, and the like, use the full spectrum of tasks from initial detailed analysis of the problem components to the field installation of the final product. Some projects are for pieces of what might become a bigger project or are for specific goals that do not require the full range of tasks required in more complex projects. No matter how big or small your project is, there are certain common elements for you to consider. The questions to resolve, as stated in Table 3-6, are the issues that will come up during most projects. The answers you choose, because of the lack of certainty about their "rightness," all involve an element of risk. As the project manager, you must help your project team and stakeholders remember the risks, and do what you can in your approach to minimize that risk.

Table 3-6. Questions to Resolve: Implementation Stage

✓	Questions	Possible Solutions
	1. What project approach will we use	• Successive analysis design, development, testing spirals • Rapid prototyping
	2. How can the tasks be distributed and assigned?	• Joint, integrated analysis/ design/development/testing teams
	3. What kinds of task areas should we include?	Product development: • Business function • Work process • Content • Product technology Product deployment: • Preimplementation • Installation to operational • Postinstallation
	4. When and how do we make modifications (e.g., to plans, to goals, to design, to logistics)?	• Ongoing project activity planning • Work progress reporting and management • Cost and time reporting and management • Product and project evaluation
	5. How will the work teams coordinate their efforts and communicate results?	• Work progress reporting and management • Project communications system management
	6. How to we know if we're still within our planned time and budget?	• Cost and time reporting and management
	7. Where is the risk and how do we combat it?	• Risk assessment and management
	8. How do we gain acceptance and adoption of our new product?	• Change process management
	9. Whom do we need to have on the team at this point in our project?	• Staff acquisition, development, and management
	10. What resources do we need to complete this part of our project?	• Resource acquisition and management
	11. What technology do we need to complete our work on this part of the project?	• Process technology acquisition, development, and management

Project Approach

. . . any real engineer knows it's impossible to understand everything without designing, building, and busting experimental devices.

—G. Harry Stine (1995, 10)

So now that we know where we are going, what we're supposed to produce, and how we will work together, now what? As the ad says, "just do it" (apologies to Nike). Or, maybe not. . . . Kathy Kozel, in a recent article in *Multimedia Producer*, called this approach the "just make it" or JMI model (1996, 84). She points out that this model, although popular with the creativity-driven producers, can lead to lots of risk and stress, much more than most of us are willing or able to tolerate. The antidote to this kind of chaos is organized structure, right?

Maybe not. Separating project work into neat, sequential steps hasn't worked all that well, either. The classic waterfall development methodology groups work into linear blocks of activity (analysis, design, development, testing), but because the activity blocks stretch out over time, the lessons learned in testing and trials are far removed from the design modification steps, limiting any practical revisions until the next development cycle. Not to mention, there are huge risks involved in developing a product based on opportunities and commitments made weeks, months, or maybe years before the actual production begins.

We, as well as the many project managers we spoke with and read about, have found other ways to organize project work. What we suggest is an approach to project work that incorporates the essence of the spiral development models and rapid prototyping models from software and systems engineering and includes the critical element of risk assess-

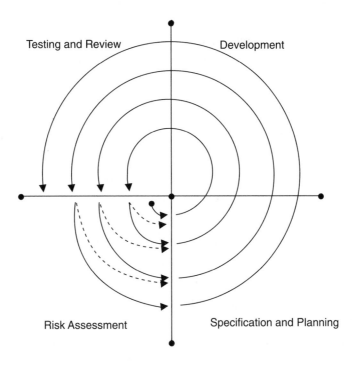

Figure 3-9. Project Management Implementation Stage Spirals

ment. These general strategies for development are the ones we have seen work most successfully in a wide range of projects. As shown in Figure 3-9, our implementation activities are arranged in spirals. Each turn of the spiral includes tasks that are needed to move the product development forward toward its desired goal. Each spiral should result in a version of the final desired product, with each successive spiral product being more complete and more ready to deploy than the previous one. How many spirals are needed depends upon how far away the final goal is and how much can be accomplished in a single turn of the spiral.

All spirals begin with assessment of the risks involved in completing this phase of product development. We agree with Boehm (1988) that identifying and doing the riskiest activities first reduce the costs if something goes wrong. To the oft quoted adage that says: You can pays me now or you can pays me later, we would add: But, it costs more if you pays me later. The next tasks in the spiral should encompass whatever is necessary to specify how the product should be constructed. These tasks will, and should, overlap with the next tasks, which are the ones required to build and test a prototype of the product. The completion of the spiral is the review and testing of the prototype to see how it performs relative to the stated goals and objectives, as well as how it meets whatever other requirements have been added by the implementation teams, based on what they have learned so far.

For example, in multimedia development there is a great deal of effort spent on constructing the various elements that make up the multimedia, the video segments, the audio bits, the animated graphics, and the interface design. Key to how these should be constructed are the decisions about what software and hardware are going to be used, as well as how the various components work together. Often a portion of the project team works on figuring out the technical side of the prototype while another group works on the content and design of it. To keep the two groups working together, we suggest that in the first spiral of development both groups should concentrate on building and testing little bits and pieces of the system and then integrate their efforts right away. Thus they can find out if the technology will do what they hope it can; for example, if a screen showing a video segment can have an audio loop as well as a small graphic that can animate (such as an arrow pointing out things to see in the video). If not they can find another program and try again. When all the little pieces are working, the team moves to the next spiral of development to put them together, constructing a small but complete module of the desired multimedia system and checking it against the overall project requirements as well as against what they learned and modified in the first tests. This process should continue through the development of the rest of the product as the team continuously checks its progress against the original project requirements and goals.

G. Harry Stine, in an article in *Analog* (May 1994, 64-73), recounts the story of the second flight of the Delta Clipper DC-X (the experimental version) on September 11, 1993. The Delta Clipper project team is attempting to build the next generation, reusable space launch vehicle. Their constraints: build it cheap and fast ($60 million in 21 months), without spending ". . . one thin dime on R & D" (1994, 66). They had to do it with available, existing technology and equipment. Stine delightedly calls the DC-X "a junkyard rocket." Why is Stine so thrilled with this project? Because it is the classic systems development project, done the right way according to most engineers and a few of the rest of us converts to this way of thinking. The right way? Build a little, break it, learn from your mistakes and problems. Build it better next time, and so on.

Software designers will recognize the rapid prototyping methodology in this description. In rapid prototyping, the project team builds an initial prototype and presents it to the customer to get immediate customer and user reaction. For example, if the project team is developing a software manual, the customer can react to a draft layout and a chapter that illustrates the page layout, graphics, and so on. At this stage, the project team can easily integrate changes that reflect the customer's preferences into the initial and subsequent chapters. As work proceeds, the project team continues to submit samples for review and makes suggested changes. In this way, the customer takes ownership of the product throughout the life of the project, and the final product is easily approved, without the need for costly revisions. Stine, and many other science fact and fiction writers over the past 40 or so years, keeps reminding us that although designing and building devices in which people are involved can be risky and difficult, the only way to find out if they work is to build them.

Stine describes the two approaches that have evolved for technology development projects. One is the classical engineering approach that calls for the building and testing of one or more experimental devices to learn whether the design calculations and concepts are sound, what and how complex systems interactions occur, whether or not anything has been overlooked in the design and construction process, and how novel technology performs in this arrangement (1995, 4-5). (These sound like great review criteria to us.) The other approach to designing new technology has evolved since World War II: Study it carefully first, understand everything, then build a final operational device (1995, 5). Those of you who have had to build project plans around the idea of delivering operational products without first testing them out can recognize the current popularity of this approach. Stine much prefers the first, classical approach, citing the Delta Clipper project as the latest example of why this "build it, break it, then rebuild it better" approach works. Henry Petroski, in *To Engineer Is Human: The Role of Failure in Successful Design* (1992), states his belief in this approach, writing:

> Because man is fallible, so are his constructions, however. Thus the history of structural engineering, indeed the history of engineering in general, may be told in its failures as well as in its triumphs. Success may be grand, but disappointment can often teach us more.

Our recommended implementation spirals obviously embrace the notion of "build it, break it, then rebuild it better" or as Kathy Kozel (1996, 86) calls it, "build a little, test a little." This approach builds in ongoing risk assessment, asking questions regularly, such as these:

- Is this the right thing?
- Does it do what it was supposed to do?
- Does it still meet our initial requirements?
- If not, has the environment in which we established those requirements changed?
- How shall we proceed based on the current situation and our reassessment of the future?

The key to making these spirals work is to set parameters for completion of each spiral. These parameters should include a clear statement of what decisions will be made based on the results of the spiral and who will be involved in making them. It should also include the criteria by which those decisions will be made. You and your project team, through your work tasks, will work to collect, analyze, and provide the right information for the decision makers. If the decision makers are involved in the actual development work—as we recommend—this process becomes much easier and quicker than it might seem at the outset.

Who Should Be Involved?

Implicit in this model is the assumption of joint, integrated teams doing the implementation tasks. In systems engineering these are called joint application development (JAD) teams; they consist of systems designers, programmers, users, business function managers, and the project manager. This integrated team membership can be used on virtually any project. The rule is to involve as many of the stakeholders as possible in the actual development of the product, whether in the actual construction of the product or in the review and testing of that product. Virtually every example we have heard or read about or experienced that did not include a cross-section of stakeholders in the implementation failed in some fashion, whether by not meeting project process goals of time and budget, or in terms of product acceptance and use.

The key stakeholder to focus on during the implementation stage, in terms of ongoing project risk mitigation, is the user or product customer. Why? It is critical to involve the user in prototype testing and reviews; otherwise time and resources will be wasted in creating a product no one will use. And, if you develop something your target users cannot or will not use, your project will fail, as we have shown in several examples in earlier sections of this book. Does this conflict with the advice we gave you in the last section about concentrating your attention on the sponsor? Not really. The sponsor needs to know the effect of the product on the user and customer. It is unlikely that the sponsor would withdraw funding from a project that is desired and used by the target customers and users, as long as their needs still fit within the organization's mission and goals.

How Do We Decide to Proceed?

The final test of the rightness of any decision to proceed or not is the question, Is this still the right project and product for the opportunity identified? This is where linkage between the sponsors' concerns and the users' concerns takes place. The "Do we proceed" question also asks that you integrate all that you have learned in the project so far, reassess the origins of the project and the analysis and decisions made during the opportunity stage and the commitment stage, before continuing forward on the project. We have found that when this is not done at regular intervals, the projects get out of control quickly. Uncertainty and change begin to wreak their havoc on the project plans, and before you know it, the project is so far over time and budget that it is hard to figure out how to recover. The FAA Advanced Automation System project described in chapter 2 is only one of the many examples we know of this. In a recent multimedia training program development project each module cost approximately $7,000 more and took an average of three months longer to develop than was planned. When user testing occurred too late in the development timeline, the subsequent revisions were much more substantial than they would have been if users had been involved earlier in the project. If they had been, better decisions could have been made on how to proceed. These are smaller numbers than the more than $3 billion that the FAA lost, but still significant to the customer and contractors involved.

Each implementation spiral of activity, whether it is an early prototype spiral or a product installation spiral will have to be planned in detail at the end of each preceding spiral. To do detailed planning all at once at the beginning of the implementation stage, while you are developing your overall project plans in the commitment stage, is to ask for trouble. Instead, we recommend that you look at your project as a series of successive approximations. You won't know exactly what is needed to be done next until the previous approximation, or prototype, is built. Further, by the time you get it built, the situation will have changed, potentially changing the need and the opportunity. Don't fight this uncertainty. No matter how much planning and thinking about it you do, you will not prevent change from happening.

Project Management and Administration During Implementation

So, what do you do to manage and administer your project? Lots of things; for example:

- Ongoing project activity planning.
- Work progress reporting and management.
- Cost and time reporting and management.

- Ongoing product and project evaluation.
- Stakeholder communications and management.
- Risk assessment and management.
- Change process management.
- Staff acquisition, development, and management.
- Resource acquisition and management.
- Process technology acquisition, development, and management.

How you do each of these items is contingent upon a number of factors, not the least of which are the type and size of your organization and the kinds of existing systems with which you must interact. No matter how big or little your organization, we have found this list includes the minimum set of relevant issues that you will need to attend to during your project. Many of the books and articles we list in the bibliography provide detailed descriptions of methodologies and approaches to use for most of the items we have listed. We will not attempt to discuss them in detail here. Our only caution to you is to consider the effect of uncertainty, change, and risk on the approach you use for things such as cost control or activity planning. We will talk more about some of the specific things you can do in the areas of stakeholder communications, resource, change, and risk management to improve your project's chances of success in later chapters of the book.

Conclusion Stage

How do you know when you're done? And furthermore, how do you move on to the next project? If you are anything like us, you have had more than a few projects end when they were overrun by others. That approach might be fine for the project team member or manager, but does little for the continued use of the project results by the organization. We rec-

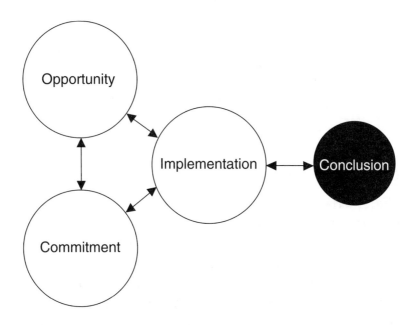

Figure 3-10. Project Management Stages: Conclusion

ommend that you prepare for the conclusion stage just as you do any other stage in project management: figure out what needs to happen, then be ready to do it when the time comes. Concluding activities can include, among other things, a final briefing and demonstration of project products; a videotape showing the services in use; and a photo session with customer staff and project team to give all those who worked to accomplish the project outcomes a tangible reminder of a successful experience. These kinds of activities signal that the project is over and that additional work will require a new contract and additional funding and resources. You should, of course, remember to modify your original ideas for conclusion stage activities based on what you know at this point in the project, not be tied to ideas and recommendations made long before the project was completed. Table 3-7 lists the questions that we like to resolve at the end of our projects. They guide our selection of project conclusion activities.

Table 3-7. Questions to Resolve: Conclusion Stage

✔	Questions
	1. How do we get final approval and acceptance of the project results?
	2. What kind of documentation do we need to leave or provide?
	3. How do we transfer the technology skills and knowledge used by the project team to the operational users?
	4. How do we say goodbye?

Get Final Approval

The criteria for the final product approval were probably generated in both the commitment stage and the implementation stage. These approval criteria should be revisited regularly at each implementation stage spiral to make sure the terms of approval are still the same, or if not, to identify how they have changed. Your task is to make sure those approval criteria are known and agreed to by the relevant stakeholders throughout the project. When you and the team believe your product meets those criteria, you should provide some written form of documentation to assert that. This is usually a memo or letter provided with the delivered product. The project client or sponsor should be asked to formally agree, through a signature and date, that the product has been received and approved. Without this formality, you may find yourself being asked for additional work or modifications to work that are really beyond the scope of your original project.

After all our earlier suggestions about *nonspecific* work plans, you may find this kind of detailed recommendation out of character. We would assure you that it is totally in keeping with our primary set of project questions. Admittedly, the specific details of how the end product will look and operate will be developed and modified as you move through the project. However, you should always be driving to a specific project result, the "what are we trying to accomplish?" and the "how will we know when we get there?" questions. When you "get there" you are, or should be, done with the project. If you want to be sure that your project process and project results are evaluated on the correct terms, you need to formally stop the project and begin the operational use of the product. Without this formal stopping point you will never be able to provide detailed facts to support your claims of a successful project.

The risk is that your project client or sponsor, or even some other stakeholder, does not formally approve the final product, leaving you open to more work requests or complaints. You should have minimized the risk of that happening through the techniques and strategies we described earlier in the other stages of the project. Help yourself. Remember to establish final approval criteria as early as you can reasonably do so in the project. Make sure they are agreed to by all the people that will need to approve the final product. If you do that, when you get to this stage, you will avoid the risk of nonapproval.

Complete Documentation and Transfer Technology

Making sure that the user organization can and will use the final product is an important task in the conclusion stage. If you have followed our suggested approach so far, you will already have involved the user organization in the implementation activities, so some of your work in this area is already done. What you must do to finish up is make sure that all the documentation describing how to use the product and how to modify it or create it over again is recorded and delivered to the appropriate organizational location. The terms of what kind of documentation, for what purposes, and for which locations will be developed and refined during the implementation stage. For example, in international projects, documentation may have to be translated into different languages, and implementation strategies may be different, depending on each country's culture. If you are clever and have been thinking about the end results from the beginning of the project, you will have built in time to develop and test this documentation along with the actual product. This step is then merely a final edit and production step.

The technology transfer issue is related. If the operation and maintenance of the product require knowledge and skills of a specific technology, then part of your activities should include the transferring of that knowledge and those skills from the project team to the target organizations. This can include such methods as developing online systems help, developing on-line or print procedures manuals, developing and conducting user training, and developing and conducting train-the-trainer workshops for those in the organization who need to teach the skills to others in the organization. A common example in systems development projects is to develop a full range of performance support materials (i.e., documentation, training, job aids) for both users and administrators of the new system and to conduct a train-the-trainer workshop for the in-house trainers of users of the new system.

These documentation and transfer activities often happen at various times over the course of a project, because these tasks must be done for more than one project deliverable. Keep track of the specific requirements for documentation and technology transfer, so that you don't get surprised by it later. When involved in multimedia or computer-based training (CBT) projects, for example, we have learned to ask up front if our team is expected to teach the in-house people how to design and develop multimedia or CBT. We have had too many experiences where that was assumed, but not specified until much later in the project, making it very difficult for us to find the time and resources necessary to meet the request. Our suggestion? Ask about the assumptions on this early, so that you can build in the necessary tasks along with other project tasks throughout the implementation.

Say Good-bye

Announcing that a project is over can be a very emotional time for both the client organization and the project team. If the project has been managed as we have suggested throughout this chapter, you will have become integrated into the organization in many ways and through many connections. The organization needs to know and formally communicate to all involved that this project has come to an end and you and your team are no longer operating. How that is done is often dependent upon the culture and style of the client organization. It could be as formal as an all-hands meeting announcement, or as informal as a Friday afternoon barbecue. Or, in an even less public way, in a letter or e-mail to the appropriate people.

You as the project manager should help your client plan the appropriate project closeout notices or events for the client organization. Remind them that this is a way for organizations that no longer seem to value long-time service to offer their appreciation for the work they now do value— project work. The project conclusion should help engender future support for other projects if handled appropriately. If some formal good-bye ceremony or notice doesn't take place, the risk is that others in the organization will not realize that the project is over, potentially causing all sorts of problems in resource management and work planning for other projects.

How you and your project team say good-bye is your decision. We do recommend that you do formally thank everyone on the team for their assistance and effort during the project. You might want to plan a celebration or send-off event to commemorate the project's end. For example, for the more than 200 volunteers in a year-long project to put on the annual conference of her (and our) professional society, the conference project manager budgeted at the start of the project for a close-out activity, and at project end, staged a thank you picnic, providing food and drink (a blessed change from the thousand times when the project team members had to be responsible for providing the refreshments). Certificates of appreciation from the society were presented, custom crafted for the occasion, most including a reference to the most difficult challenge faced and met by that volunteer. The stories exchanged by the team members, many of whom had been too busy to notice what anyone else had been doing, provided more than enough entertainment to keep the party going for hours. The specifics of this event were not planned until after the project was completed, but early budgeting of an amount to conduct some sort of closing activity is an excellent idea for all project managers.

The long-term payoff for having a formal good-bye ceremony of some sort is often in having people who are willing to work with you and each other again. These events create a sense of having been involved in something that created or completed something, a feeling that we do not get from much of our work activities. At the very least, we suggest that you, as the project manager, should meet with each of the team members as they leave the project to give and receive feedback on the conduct of the project. You can learn a lot about how to better manage your team by finding out what worked well and what didn't work so well for each of your team members. Use the good-bye formality as the way to make sure you get that feedback.

Summary

This chapter has laid out an approach to planning and managing projects that recognizes and embraces the absolute certainty that uncertainty will frame and produce many of a project's processes, outputs, and results. This approach also recognizes that the criteria for success of a project will be different in each project and for each organization. The criteria for success of using this approach, however, is always the same: that you and the project team deliver the project outputs and achieve the expected results according to the established project success criteria. How? By learning to live and breathe comfortably in an atmosphere of change and uncertainty. By staying clear about what results are desired in your project, and staying practical and flexible about how you go about trying to achieve them. By thinking, What is the risk? in conjunction with all planning and decision-making activities. By helping your clients, customers, and other project stakeholders learn to live with uncertainty and risk, and to deal with them flexibly.

An impossible set of tasks? No. Most of what is required is the recognition that you cannot control, absolutely, the project process or results. What you, the project manager, need to learn and use are the skills, knowledge, and strategies of this approach so that you can avoid uncertainty and risk where you can and identify and mitigate it where you can't. This should naturally lead to more successful projects, as judged by whatever criteria you care to use. The next few chapters provide more specific examples and guidelines for applying those new skills and strategies.

Chapter **4**

The Project Manager as Politician

Never forget that all projects are political.

—Arthur Gingrande (1994)

Projects follow a quantum model—interaction and observation create reality. As a project manager, you create and observe a myriad of interactions, all of which change the reality surrounding the project. Your responsibility is to make sure you and everyone associated with the project stay aware of those changes in the project reality and of the part they play, personally, in changing that reality. You need to make and expand connections that ensure that you will receive feedback from everyone who has a stake in your project, so that you *can* anticipate and respond to changes, both expected and unexpected. You can't be an effective project manager if you just concentrate on defining and completing technical work. Relationships are the key to project success. If critical relationships are not established, no matter how well the project work is done, there is risk that you will not satisfy the customer, and the project will be perceived as a failure. Frequently, the difference between success and failure is the quality of the relationships the project manager develops.

To be a successful project manager, you need to be, in the best sense, a politician. You need to build a constituency for your project, identifying and recognizing supporters and winning over those whose support you do not yet have. You need to build a network.

Networking

Project managers must first scan the environment and decide who should be in their network. Take as your model the small business owners in your community. They forge networks that include community and service groups, other business owners, clients, and suppliers. This is a survival strategy for a business. Networking is also a survival strategy for a project manager.

What a Network Is

Networks are informal structures that provide members with three major benefits (Carter 1996):

- Information about available resources and potential problems.
- Support, in the form of encouragement, recognition, and coalition building.
- Access to individuals and organizations.

Networks are based on cooperation, not competition. They are not power relationships but are more like barter—the exchange of things of value. The difference is that the payback does not have to be immediate and may be made to any network member, because a network exists for the benefit of all its members. For example, you may refer a job applicant to another project manager with a need for the applicant's skills. This creates goodwill that you can draw upon later.

In the role of politician, you will build and maintain support for your project by forming networking relationships with all those who have a stake in it (as described in chapter 3), including:

- Sponsors who can commit resources and funding.
- Advocates who can influence the commitment of resources and funding and who will be involved in or affected by the project implementation.
- Technical or subject matter experts who will help you with development and review project work.
- Product customers or end users who will use what you produce.
- Suppliers or subcontractors who will be providing services or supplies to support the project effort.
- Project team members who come from within or outside of the organization to work on parts or all of the project activities.

The importance of networking in project management success was shown by the results of a major research study on project management sponsored by NASA (Baker, Murphy and Fisher 1974). The research showed that some projects were perceived as successful even though they failed two critical tests: they were not completed on time, and they were not completed within budget. The research showed that, "Next to technical performance and satisfaction of those associated with, and affected by a project, effective coordination and relation patterns are the most important contributors to perceived project success."

The risk is that your project can pass the two critical tests (on time, within budget) and even the third critical test (achieves intended results), and still be perceived as a failure. A project report at a conference talked about creating computer-based simulation training for pilots of a new aircraft. The pilots completed the performance testing that followed the training and passed with flying (sorry) colors.

However, even several weeks and months later, when asked for feedback about the training, the pilots said the training was inadequate. The fact that they could actually fly the plane had seemingly no effect on their feelings that the training hadn't done the job. In this case, the end users, the pilots, felt that the best training should be in a classroom and in an actual airplane. Because neither of those two elements were included in the computer-based tutorials and simulations, they judged it as inadequate. The project team should have done more to change the expected reality for their end users before they tried to force those users to accept it.

Relating to All the Stakeholders

Even before you commit to a project, you need to analyze the political situation critically to identify all the stakeholders and establish relationships with them. Some of the questions and issues you need to examine for each of the stakeholder groups are provided in the next paragraphs. A project manager who is a good politician will get answers to these questions and issues before committing to a project and will continue to keep them in mind as the project goes forward.

Sponsors

- Who is or are the real sponsors of this project? Remember, follow the money. The sponsor is the one paying for or funding the project. Often there are several sponsors, and the individual or group that initiates the contact with you may be a customer or advocate who has only limited authority or influence to commit funds and resources. You will need to be careful not to spend more time satisfying these intermediaries than you do in satisfying the true sponsor, client, or customer, of the project.

- Why does the sponsor think the project is needed? Is there any data to support the need? Is the data convincing or persuasive to the sponsor? How exactly to present this kind of data must also be considered. For example, the fact that other organizations have achieved results in similar projects can be either a big boost to your credibility and encourage the implementation of a similar project, or it can be an obstacle that needs to be overcome by redesigning the project so that it doesn't look exactly like the other organization's project. Without knowing how your sponsor will react, you will be unable to guess, except by chance (how's that for uncertainty?), which approach will best solicit your sponsor's support.
- What's in it for the sponsor? The project should reflect a business need or organizational goal; if it does not, the uncertainty factor is very high. The sponsors will probably have a good idea of the kind of business results they are expecting. Make sure you know what these are and explain how the project will contribute to them. Key sponsors also need to see how they will benefit personally. This is known as the WIIFM factor—What's In It For Me? If the sponsors are not personally affected—or will be adversely affected—by the project, the risk is high that their support will erode over time.

Advocates or Champions

- Who are the decision makers who, although they cannot commit funds, will oversee the project, will contribute resources to the project, and can accept or reject the project products or services? How will you interact with them? These people usually have influence on the sponsors as well as on others in the organization who will be supporting or implementing the project. Depending on the project, they can include managers of affected or related depart-

ments, technical or subject matter experts, union representatives, or quality control managers.

- Have you or anyone in your network had experience with
these people? Was it negative or positive? Who were the individuals involved? Based on this experience, which of these
people or groups are likely to support you? Who will not?
- What will a good project outcome look like from the perspective of each of these decision makers and influencers?
If they are in conflict about the desired outcome, you may
not be able to satisfy all of them. For example, in one of
Lori's projects, a major improvement was made to an
information system that provided headquarters managers
with very important data. However, the system also generated much more work for the field staffs, who had not been
involved in developing the system. The field staffs, predictably, were unwilling to increase their workload and did
their best to sabotage the project.

Technical or Subject Matter Experts

- Who can provide the project team with needed technical
or subject matter information and support? How available
are they likely to be? If you cannot get answers to critical
technical questions, you may be unable to meet project
timelines.
- How willing or able are they to contribute to the project? If
you cannot get accurate or complete information about the
work or content being developed by the project, the quality, and therefore the ultimate acceptability, of the final
product will be jeopardized.

Product Customers or End Users

- Who will use the products or services the project creates?
Can they be available to try out prototypes? Have they

been involved in the decision to initiate the project? Will they be adversely affected by the project outcomes? What benefits can you identify for them?

Suppliers, Vendors, Subcontractors

• What products and services will be required to complete the project? Are there any restrictions on sources you can use? Are there price limitations that may influence the quality of goods and services you can obtain? How do you plan to identify the resources you will need?

Project Team Members

• Who are these people and where did they come from? Are they members of the sponsor, advocate, technical, subject matter, or customer or end-user organizations? Do they have particular goals, or hidden agendas, that they will be trying to advance? Will those agendas jeopardize the project?

• Are the project team members capable and willing to participate in the project? Are they interested in doing the project right or in just getting the project done? Does this project contribute to their personal growth and development goals? How can this project contribute to their personal goals?

All of these stakeholder groups are the project manager's customers or clients. It is important to stay clear about the distinction between the customers or clients of the project, and the customer of the project's products. The customer or end user of the project's products is only one component of the overall project manager's customer or client. All of the stakeholders described here are different components or levels of the project's customer, and as a project manager you need to try to satisfy all of them. Therefore, make sure you don't concentrate all your efforts on one group of customers, at the risk of alienating or ignoring another group. You need all of these groups with you in order for the project to succeed. Think of it as creating a shared reality. The more the various stakeholders contribute to the creation of the project, the more they contribute to and become aware of the changed reality. How can they reject the reality they have personally assisted in creating? This is the job of the politician project manager—to help all the stakeholders feel as if they served an important role in creating that new reality, while at the same time getting them to actually do it.

Create a Partnership

The experience of the project managers we have talked with confirms our own experience that the client or customer should be a partner, never an adversary or just the recipient of finished work. Customers need to know that the project is as important to you as it is to them, not only because of its revenue-producing potential, but also because of the professional challenges it presents, the value it has for your customer, and the potential it offers to develop a long-term mutually beneficial relationship between you.

Bob Hunter (1996), a partner in Anderson Consulting with many years of project management experience, voices the philosophy of most successful project managers we know. He says his firm never wants to be seen as a consultant or a vendor providing services, but as a full partner with a major stake in the project. When they first become aware of a potential project, they assess whether it will be possible to establish this kind of relationship, because experience has shown them that if either party sees the relationship as adversarial, the project is likely to fail unless this attitude can be overcome.

A partner relationship will reduce your level of risk, because it gives your customer an equal stake with you in the project success. We recommend that when you first walk across your customer's threshold, you consciously use the words *we* and *us* in place of *I* and *me*. This helps remind you and your customer that you all are on the same team, working toward shared goals. Even internal project managers need to demonstrate this partner relationship with customers in other organizational departments. Interdivisional strife and competition have caused more than one project to fail. Help your internal customers remember that you all stand to gain from a successful project just as you all will suffer the consequences of a failed one.

Establish Common Goals

> *It's like kneading bread dough.*
>
> —Amy Titus (1996)

If you want to be viewed in a positive light, as a contributor to the organization, not as an outsider, get to know your client's staff, and keep on friendly terms with people at all levels. Amy Titus, President of Titus Austin, Inc., who has extensive experience in international project management, says that in successful projects, a politically astute project manager will spend a lot of time at the client site, learning how to get along with everyone at every level, and slowly learning how to influence people. You need to have the patience to give the ideas you've presented time to germinate. "It's like kneading bread dough again and again and giving it time to rise each time," she says. But if the project manager does not lay the groundwork carefully, the project can easily unravel.

She gives the example of U.S. Agency for International Development (AID) projects that provide money to countries to meet objectives that further U.S. policies. Countries want the funds, but they will only do what will not put them at risk with their own constituencies. A wise project manager, in this instance, will be wary of a country's agreement to the project goals and will carefully and continually assess the situation to be sure that the project goals are really accepted—not just given lip service in order to get available funds. Titus suggests two strategies to accomplish this. First, the project manager needs to maintain an ongoing dialogue with country representatives, so that she is continually aware of any departure from the project goals. Second, the project manager needs to make routine checks, to ensure that the resources (e.g., time of expert advisors and space and facilities) that were promised for the project are actually being committed.

Acceptance of the project goal is critical in international aid projects because U.S. officials want the people in the country to sustain the project activities after the project ends and the project team disbands. But, unless the project really was politically acceptable, it will face a very uncertain future after the project staff goes home. Titus says that the key to lasting success is to align the project goals with the client's values. Clients must see the project as being in their own interest. If they accept the project goals only because of pressure to get funds or to comply with what they perceive to be a fad of the moment, the project cannot succeed.

Titus described a project she directed to train field workers to disseminate family planning techniques in communities in one developing country. The training needed to be practical and experiential, but a hands-on, practical training approach was alien to the culture of the country's training institutions. Educators from the country who were assigned to her project team wanted to present the training in formal classroom lectures, without the hands-on, problem-solving exercises.

Titus, in her role as the project manager, used project team meetings as coaching and counseling sessions to get the local educators to accept a different approach. When she met with the team, she listened to their concerns and then encouraged them to roleplay the situations that they felt were most problematic. This practice was their first experience with this experiential, problem-solving approach. They found that it was an interesting way to identify sources of resistance and to develop strategies to overcome them. Over time, the local educators became enthusiastic about this method of problem solving and began to accept and use activity-based instructional techniques.

Show That You Can Provide Value Added

A politically astute project manager will ensure that the project exceeds what is strictly required by the contract. When you know your customer well, you can identify value-added things you can do, often at no cost to you. For example, many customers find their physical architecture does not support a team approach very well. Meeting space for the teams is often in very short supply. If this is true for your customer, offer to make your conference room available, or help find them space for project work perhaps in another facility or in another organization's training or conference space.

One of the things Business Reengineering Resources, Inc. (BRRI) provides to all of its clients is the documentation of all decision making and product development that takes place during reengineering project team meetings. Taking on the burden of documenting the results of the work endears BRRI to its clients at the same time it makes it possible to proceed with the project most efficiently. This adds value to the relationship from both partners' points of view.

Give your customer the value of your past experience. You may have done similar work in the past that is relevant to the new project, or you may know of similar work that was already done in another part of your customer's own organization. Share this information. It will be very valuable to the customer. We have been amazed, particularly when the customer is a large corporate organization or a government agency, at how often information about various projects and their results is not communicated across organizational units. We predict this will be increasingly the case, as work is outsourced to individual projects replacing entire functions that formerly were done in-house and as work continues to be done through project teams that disband when the project is completed, leaving little institutional memory of what was done in different project tasks. Organizations who have not yet established processes for documenting and transmitting this kind of information will definitely appreciate anything you can share in this regard.

Another value to provide to your customer is your saying, "Some project tasks duplicate previously done work. We can save time and money if we incorporate this existing data and concentrate our efforts on what is specific to this effort." This increases the level of confidence in you, at the same time giving your project the benefit of products that have already been reviewed and used. Sometimes, adapting existing work also provides you with new opportunities to add to your network experts who can provide valuable insights gleaned from their past experience.

Demonstrating appreciation of value can go both ways in the customer partnership. Anderson Consulting invites its most satisfied clients to a special event each year to celebrate their successful working relationships. While you and your team might not be able to afford that level of appreciation, other smaller actions can show how much you value your relationship. For example, if a customer is visiting from out of town, take time to check that their lodgings are at a location that is convenient to your office and provide information they will need about transportation food and the like. This will help them to make the most efficient use of their time at your site and ensure that they have a less stressful experience. One project manager we know always has food and beverages available on the first day of meeting, particularly if some of the project team and customers have had to travel in to the meeting. Another project team provided an open house, complete with refreshments, for the customer to celebrate the completion of a prototype. It's not the size of gesture that counts. What counts is that it is a genuine reflection of your appreciation of the value of the partnership relationship.

Placing a Monetary Value on Value Added

In some types of projects, it may even be possible to place a monetary value on the value added. Anderson Consulting has a policy they call value building. They establish the value of the project with the client and reach agreement with the client on how value will be measured. Then if the project exceeds this level of value, the client agrees to pay a percentage of the increased value generated, for example 10 percent, to Anderson Consulting. This benefits both parties; Anderson Consulting gets 10 percent of the added value, and the client enjoys 90 percent.

Taking Leadership Responsibility

To be a partner with your customer, you need to keep alert to their changing needs and priorities. But this does not mean that you can be nondirective and let the client take charge of the project. It is your responsibility to lead the effort. Your political challenge in an open, collaborative partnership is to do this in a way that carefully keeps all stakeholders in the loop and in an appropriate relationship to the project. In our project management model, roles and turf are agreed to by all stakeholders at the project start during the commitment stage, and everyone should continue to accept the responsibilities they were assigned, unless the agreement is changed. Research on why projects are perceived as successful shows that a major factor is the extent to which the project manager was seen to be in control (Baker, Bruce and Murphy 1974).

Staffing Decisions

Customers often want to make decisions about the selection of project staff; this can be a delicate matter that requires good use of your political skills. If you are an internal project manager and will be getting your project team from within the organization, you will, of course, need to work with the customer to secure project staff. You should agree at the outset on ground rules about this and then monitor it as the project progresses. For example, who makes the final decision on who should serve on the team? Must you take everyone who is offered, or can you select from them to construct the best team? Is the staff available as needed, or is the home organization making conflicting demands on the individual's time?

As an external project manager, your agreement about project staff will probably be different. You will want to retain rights to make final selection decisions for the staff you bring to the customer's project. However, you may agree that the customer will have the opportunity to interview and approve key personnel for a specific project. You also may agree that if the client is dissatisfied with the performance of a specific staff member, you will investigate their concern and take appropriate action. Acceptance of staff is always especially critical if the project staff works at the customer's site where a smooth working relationship is more important than in projects where the customer interfaces directly only with the project manager and key project task managers.

However, as project manager you are ultimately responsible for the work of the project team; you need to have the freedom to select team members who have the skill and experience and the salary requirements that the project requires and the budget can support. You also need to develop strategies to deal with client complaints about project staff that sometimes violate even the customer's own published policies. For example, one project manager told us that a customer complained to him that the women on the project staff were not sufficiently deferential to males on the customer staff. Another issue might be that older, experienced project staff members may need to maintain a low profile with a customer who is very young and may be more comfortable with people closer to his or her own age. In dealing with these preferences, you, as the project manager, need to tactfully keep the focus on the tasks to be done, and how people are doing them. Remember that your reputation for fairness is also involved and will follow you throughout your career.

Get to Know the Customer's Technical and Subject Matter Experts

If you can, meet the technical and subject matter experts who will be available to provide information to the project staff. Find out what their work schedules are and when they are most likely to be available. When you talk with them, let them know what you will need from them and when, and make them aware that access to their expertise will be very important to your team. Tell them about your team members who will be working with them. Establishing a good rapport with these experts mitigates the risk that they will be unavailable when you need them. Make sure you give feedback to them and their home office managers about the value they provide to the project. Don't forget to show appreciation and consideration for the time these people are made available to the project. Thank-you notes are never inappropriate. (Miss Manners is a politician at heart!)

Keep the End User in the Loop

You will mitigate risk if you involve representative users of the products and services developed by your project as early in the project as possible. The risk of neglecting to do this is high. The General Services Administration (GSA) in its recent paper, "Information Technology Projects: Keys to Success", said that in government integrated resources management (IRM) projects, user involvement in the development, implementation, and management of systems beginning in the pilot stage is critical. When users are not involved, systems are developed that do not meet the real needs of the system users. Conversely, when users are involved from the beginning, they help identify problems and suggest solutions. Learn from this. You should involve users in the initial stages of the project (opportunity and commitment) and keep them involved as each prototype is developed (implementation stage). Their feedback is critical. Projects that develop new software solutions frequently do not achieve the anticipated productivity improvements because users are given insufficient exposure to the software before it is introduced in the workplace.

Kathy Kozel, writing in *Multimedia Producer* (1996), says handcuffing the programmer to the user throughout the product development would be the ideal solution. That is unrealistic, but scheduling numerous small user tests throughout the entire production cycle avoids ". . . being shocked by user feedback . . . when it's far too late to do anything but fix bugs."

An Example from Real Life

One project in which Lori participated as a designer involved vast amounts of rewriting and redesigning a series of multimedia modules based on the review comments of a group of specialists in training, video, graphical design, and systems, who were not system users. When the modules were ultimately shown to the users, they were rejected for a series of reasons, none of which had been identified by the intermediary group. The project team designers might still have had to make changes based on the comments of both groups, but it would have been much more efficient to make them all at once. The project team also could have lessened the dueling reviewers syndrome, a phenomenon that seems to take place all too often in projects, where reviewers disagree and the project is stalled until a satisfactory resolution is agreed on, as happened in this case. In this example, the users also lost respect and credibility in the intermediary group, damaging future relations on other projects. This is not the result that you, as a project manager, want to leave behind your project work. As a project manager you need to give critical attention to ensuring that you get feedback from end users or you will waste scarce project resources in the resulting revision cycles.

Identify User Training Requirements Early

As a project manager, you need to be sensitive to the political advantage of being able to roll out a product that people can immediately use. This will only be possible if you have identified the training needed and provided it before the product rollout. The GSA recommends that training issues be identified early, so that end users receive the training they need, both on the new application the project team is developing and on changes to the business process the application supports. A way to do this is to use your first prototypes to identify training needs and then develop and field test the training in successive prototypes. You should also field test at all the user sites, to identify unique user needs at different locations.

Make Your Suppliers and Subcontractors Your Partners

In most projects suppliers and subcontractors of goods and services, such as hardware or software vendors, temporary employee services, and video conference facility managers, make critical contributions to project tasks. As James Moore points out in his book, *The Death of Competition* (1996), suppliers should be viewed as partners. Your relationship with your suppliers and subcontractors should mirror the collegial relationship you want to have with your own customer.

Select suppliers and subcontractors with care. Check references and work samples. Let them know that you have selected them because of their good reputations and quality products or services. Establish ongoing relationships with them and give them advance notice of when you will need them and exactly what you will need from them.

These people are a vital link in your political network. If they have good experiences working with you, they will keep you informed of other similar opportunities you can team on together; they will tell other potential clients that you are good people to work with. Let them know that they are in your network and that you will gladly provide references to their good work.

Be a Colleague

Look for opportunities to share ideas with everyone in your network, regardless of whether they are on you project team or not. You can share articles, books, and World Wide Web information sources on subjects you know interest them, project related or related to their hobbies or personal interests. Let them share with you, too. Borrow materials, take care of them, and return them with a note on how they were helpful to the project team. This type of goodwill goes a long way toward establishing and maintaining networking relationships within an organization.

Don't forget to consider enlisting your customer in helping you write an article or make a presentation about your project for one of your professional association meetings. We have done this numerous times over the years. It has brought us repeat business from some of those customers, as well as some unsolicited testimonials about our projects from those customers on other public speaking occasions. With one customer we put together a briefing and demonstration that we could take on the road to the organization's dispersed locations. After the trip the customer reported much more interest and support for the project from the field locations, not to mention lots more respect being accorded to her and the project team. Our future business together didn't suffer, either. The payoff for this kind of activity is uncertain at best. However, not doing things like this engender the risk of having a customer never wanting to work with you again. Besides, we have found it is always easier to work with friends.

Cultivate Influential Friends

If your project is funded on an incremental basis, it will be at risk at every budget cycle. You may periodically need to sell it, or to help your customer sell it, to the funding source to ensure a continuing revenue stream. This is always a problem with large-scale, multiyear projects. For example, FAA projects like the Advanced Automation System (AAS) need support from the airline industry to ensure continued funding, as the composition of Congress and the executive branch change, and new FAA administrators are appointed.

Industry groups like the Airline Pilots Association, the Air Traffic Controllers Association, and the Air Transport Association, which are key stakeholders in the AAS, have been powerful lobbyists for it, because they know its potential to improve air traffic control and thus reduce their operating costs and improve aviation safety. An FAA project manager and sponsor needs to work with these industry groups as well as the various executive branch and congressional decision-making bodies to get funding support continued.

But even if yours is a small project, it may have to compete for funds as budgets shrink and priorities change. Be sure to keep the sponsors, who can influence funding decisions, aware of the value of your project and the progress you are making. Invite them to project briefings; tell them in person; send them copies of progress reports. Reduce the risk that they will lose sight of your project over time. If they were enthusiastic about it at the outset, encourage their enthusiasm. If they were reluctant supporters, win them over by providing positive news of project progress, asking them for their views, and encouraging them to be involved.

Educate Your Customer

One source of risk that can be anticipated is that an uneducated customer will unwittingly request changes to the project work that will be costly and time-consuming. For example, Karen Taylor of ELF says their clients often don't know what is involved when they contract for a multimedia production. To avoid misunderstandings, ELF developed a handbook that spells out the steps and explains what each step requires of ELF and of their customer. Because the process is so technically complex, project managers give the handbook out in sections, as each part becomes relevant to the ongoing project activities. Before they did this, customers would request changes that seemed minor to them but that actually involved substantial unbudgeted cost and effort. Now when they request changes, they understand what a specific type of change entails—and what it will cost.

Delays as a Source of Risk

You will also have to educate your customers on the risks that can be caused by delays in the review of work. Because ELF projects share expensive and limited production equipment and facilities, a client delay of a day in signing off on a work plan may risk a two-week delay in the next phase if the resources needed have been previously committed for use by other projects. ELF managers have set up a whiteboard calendar that is updated regularly to be sure that everyone knows when resources are scheduled for use, who will be using them, and where.

Don't Neglect the Politics!

In your role of politician, you need to be aware of everything that may affect the success of your project, including people, technology, changes in the work environment, and changes in the sponsoring organization. The role of politician is often the most important role in project management. Don't neglect it. Don't think you shouldn't need to dabble in politics. Make politics your hobby, your avocation. If you fail to pay attention to the politics, you will fail, even if you are highly competent to deal with all the technical aspects of your project. But, if you are a highly skilled technical manager with political instincts to anticipate uncertainties and deal with the resulting risks, you are likely to be highly successful.

Chapter 5

The Project Manager as Human Resources Manager

Managing the people on your project team and facilitating the team meetings and activities are critical project manager responsibilities, because the risk of project failure is high if the project team is not competent, or motivated, to provide high-quality performance. Most projects succeed or fail in their execution depending largely on the skill, knowledge, and commitment to quality of the project team. In the model we presented in chapter 3, the project manager is a team leader among equals, in a collaborative enterprise—not an authoritarian figure with all the answers.

If you manage a project within a large organization, you will most likely have a human resources department to deal with the payroll, benefits, and other major administrative concerns of your project team members. But because you will usually be expected to manage and run the project as an entrepreneurial venture, you will have relative autonomy in planning and managing work, budget, staff selection and assignment, and resource acquisition and management. You will be a human resources manager, responsible for your own career development and the development of the people on your team during the time they work with you. You will avoid a great deal of uncertainty and risk if you do this well.

Your tasks will include deciding what skills and knowledge you need on your team at each project stage; recruiting, selecting, and hiring a team with these skills; and then creating an environment in which team members are encouraged to do their best work and motivating and coaching them so that they reach their peak performance.

Just-In-Time Staffing

Managing a project team is a major challenge, given the short-term relationship you often have with the people on your team. Project teams are volatile; flexibility is their great advantage. They can be formed as needed, expanded, or reduced just in time to match task requirements, then disbanded when the work is completed. This volatility creates a constantly shifting environment that moves internal staff people and outside consultants and vendors in and out to suit project requirements. Some of your project staff will be people who are assigned to your project only for the time it takes to complete the tasks in which they have expertise. Over the course of a year these same people have their time parceled out among several different projects. Some of these people have become "high-tech nomads" as a recent *Wall Street Journal* article labeled them. These people are "the vanguard, perhaps, of a new kind of career: the project junkie" (Wysocki 1996, A1). Regardless of whether they are internal or external, these project staffers move from project to project as outsiders without a real home. This can create some real culture clashes and trust problems between the reliable, long-term insiders and the hot-shot outsiders that will need to be dealt with if your project is going to succeed. One way to deal with this is to establish team rather than individual project assignments, so that these experts become equal partners with the internal team members over the life of the project.

The other dilemma brought about by the project mentality is that even insiders, who are assumed to have assured jobs after the project ends, feel after a while that they, like the outsider project nomads, are on their own when it comes to personal and career development. The project manager is faced with a serious task of trying to encourage project loyalty among a team of people who share little common motivation for project success.

Rich Cebula of Hughes STX (1996), discussing the transitory nature of project work, pointed to the NASA Space Shuttle project, which was ending. Pressure to meet project milestones had been intense and project scientists worked very hard to get the systems on the shuttle ready on time for the launch. Now that the project is over, these dedicated people feel the letdown. There is a widespread feeling among the project team members that people are disposable.

As a project manager, you may often be leading a team whose members have had similar experiences. You need to promote your project as a satisfying and valuable experience that will add to each team member's repertoire of skill and knowledge and make every team member a valuable addition to future project teams. The trick will be to find ways to make sure all project team members feel that they have a valuable part to play in the project, and that the end of the project is not the end to their personal value; this is a risky proposition for project managers not necessarily experienced in staff development, coaching, and counseling skills.

Precarious Funding

Funding is a source of uncertainty for most projects—especially when corporate priorities shift or profits shrink. At the start of your project, you develop a budget that provides a specific funding level for a certain period to complete the work. But when project funding is reduced, people often lose their jobs—or they may have to give up work they enjoyed. If it's a small cut, you may be able to have people reallocated to other projects. But even at Hughes STX, a 1,400-person company, this is not always possible. If your company is small, project budget cuts will usually result in layoffs, or in reduced availability of consultants and other resources.

I loved my job—losing it was like dying.

—Betsy Stalcup (1996, 6)

Project team members who are affected by cuts tend to view them as arbitrary and capricious, no matter what the circumstances, and as a project manager, you are likely to feel their anger and frustration. Project managers in these all-too-common situations must deal not only with the loss of staff to complete the project work, but also with lowered morale and feelings of threat in those who are not laid off. It is difficult to motivate people who fear they may be the next to be fired.

Margaret Kirk, writing in the *New York Times* (1995, 11), points out that those who manage to escape layoffs often also grapple with feelings of guilt. You run the risk that this will result in poor performance, unless you are able to help people envision the new results that are now possible and what actions they can take to achieve them.

Ironically, because the level of effort required by the project is rarely changed to meet the reduced staffing level, the team members that are spared must work harder and work longer hours to complete project tasks. This presents an interesting dilemma for the project manager, who often had no input into the budget decision that downsized the project.

This situation is a good time to remember that you are a team and help people to support each other. Let people grieve for their laid-off colleagues. Then work with them to get the project completed.

Lean and Mean Staffing

In former times, contracts were awarded to the lowest bidder who presented a credible work plan. Bidders were external to the organization that needed the work. Today, however, internal departments also may have to develop budgets to prove that they can do their traditional work more cost-effectively than a project team from outside the company that specializes in their type of work. Thus, as a project manager, you may be leading a corporate team, or an external team; but in either environment, you will be expected to keep staffing lean and mean.

There are several ways to do this. One common method used to achieve this goal is to hire fewer than normal entry-level people to do routine work, like spinning computer tapes and programming. But, the problem with this method is that the routine work must still be done, and responsibility for it is often forced upon higher salaried professionals. This not only presents a morale problem, but also has long-term risks. For example, your highly skilled, creative people might have used the time spent on these routine tasks to develop marketable new ideas that could result in revenue-generating projects. Try to minimize the risk of such a lost opportunity by carefully monitoring the time your skilled people spend on routine chores, and don't burden any one person with them. Darryl Sink, an experienced project manager in multimedia and systems development projects, echoed this advice in his presentation on designing in a high-change environment by encouraging us to not burden the writers with routine work duties during a project. He suggested the use of a project coordinator to off-load duties from writers (1996). Contracting for lower-paid assistants to help the higher-paid writers makes good financial sense.

Try meeting with your team to discuss with them the work that must be done and jointly work out an equitable way to do it. Through collaborative brainstorming, you may be able to develop a solution. For every example, use part-time student interns at low pay who can benefit from the opportunity to interact with experienced people in the fields they are studying. Our computer forum or listserve messages are filled with pleas from teachers and students alike looking for relevant paid and unpaid work experience.

Another method of reducing staff costs, on the other hand, is to hire many lower-paid entry-level team members, for example, to do the coding necessary for a major information technology project. Their low salaries keep project costs low while maintaining or even increasing the number of labor hours that can be committed to the effort, shortening timeframes for deliverables. But the risk is that the lack of depth and experience of these workers can create many errors and degrade product quality over the life of the project cycle. If you decide to keep labor costs low by using less-experienced people, minimize this risk by providing them with concentrated training, coaching, and a supervised apprenticeship program so that they will be able to perform efficiently and effectively. Then put a good quality control process in place and monitor quality closely.

Building a Project Team

A project team does not automatically coalesce and become productive. People on the team may be strangers or may know each other but never have worked together. Or they may have had bad experiences working together on other projects—or even in their personal lives. Your project team will be successful in working together to the extent that you are able to be an effective team leader, coaching and motivating each team member to meet the project goals. Although the team needs the benefit of every member's strengths, the team should also provide an opportunity to help each member become more proficient in areas that are new or more challenging—another tricky balance you must try to achieve.

Be a proactive manager who develops a good rapport with your team from the start. You need their buy-in and support. Deal with their uncertainty. Meet with your project team as soon as possible after the start of the project. Tell them about the project, emphasizing what they will do and what they can learn from it. Describe the need for the project. Identify the customer and how the project will benefit them. Find a time for this meeting when everyone—including graphic artists and other personnel that you share with other teams—can be available. Serve refreshments. Tell them how glad you are to be working with them. Mention the previous good work of each team member. Take a picture for the newsletter, if you have one. Have the meeting give your team a name. Let these team members tell you how they can most effectively work with you and what they need from you and other team members to provide good service.

Discuss the project goals and anticipated outcomes. Explain what is to be done and by when. Explain what the quality standards will be. Solicit input from the team to set up your work plan and establish a quality control process. Make them aware of potential risks and encourage them to accept shared responsibility for the project. If possible, divide up the work and let them bid on ownership for parts of it. In our experience, this works much better than having the project manager make unilateral decisions and announcing them.

Lori's and Mary's work nearly always involves virtual teams—that is, teams made up of people from different locations and organizations, all combining their efforts into a particular project. What they and others, such as Tim Spannaus at Emdicium and Jackie Dobrovolny of Triple Play Software who work in and manage similar far-flung project teams, have found is that an in-person, face-to-face meeting early in the project is critical to its success (Dobrovolny, Gillespie, and Spannaus 1996). These meetings develop project team-work and camaraderie, establishing work patterns and customs that will be used throughout the project. Discussions and agreements made during these initial meetings will carry much more weight than any other project information exchange, so make sure you use the time wisely to get all the major issues and risks on the table for consideration. Risk shared is always easier than risk faced alone.

Feedback

Set a time at least once a week to discuss the project and encourage team members to tell you both good news and bad news. Remember that your project is always at great risk when people don't provide useful feedback. Be sure they know you are receptive to their ideas and that they have confidence that you will not hold their opinions against them at a later date, when you yourself are under stress. When you are informed of a problem, follow through reliably to find a solution. Ask the team to suggest areas that could benefit from innovation and encourage and assist in pursuing changes that have promise. In subsequent meetings, let the team members describe how these changes are coming along and what is needed to continue them. It's important for people to feel that their ideas are being listened to, whether the team adopts them or not.

Explain how you plan to evaluate work. Tell your team as a group what your standards are and how you will provide feedback on their performance. If that feedback will include assessments from others, such as quality reviewers or editors, make sure they understand that. Promise them that you will discuss their work with them on a regular basis and that you will write a memo for their file on any substantive issues that arise. Then, follow through on your promise. This will not only be fair to the people involved, but also will make it much easier for you to justify your evaluation of their work. Be sure you repeat these assurances with individuals, and with new people who join your team.

Rewards

It is important that people on your team feel they are treated fairly. At the start of the project, define the roles, responsibilities, and rewards. Then, don't let people on your project team get lost in the shuffle as they move among project assignments. Coordinate with other project managers in whatever performance evaluation you are using to be sure that people get credit for their good work and that poor performance is also noted.

Develop a reward structure appropriate to a project environment. The transient nature of project assignments requires incentives and rewards that are motivating to people whose careers do not move in a straight vertical line but lead horizontally from project to project.

One benefit that usually costs nothing and that most people appreciate is a flexible time schedule. Karen Taylor says that at ELF, employees can work at home one day a week; one employee works off-site to be with a spouse who is completing a degree at a school in another state. Casual dress codes or special casual days are popular and cost you nothing. But be sure that people dress appropriately. You want your team to be perceived as having competence and good sense!

Pay increases may be the most difficult type of reward to provide. You will probably be under heavy pressure from the competitive marketplace, from stockholders, and in the case of government agencies, from Congress to get projects completed faster, better, and cheaper. This philosophy, together with the short-term nature of project assignments, restricts upward mobility and wage increases for many people as they move laterally from project to project, doing the same work.

You may feel that scientists and other professionals on your project who have high levels of education, advanced academic degrees, and specialized experience are not paid wages that are commensurate with that education and experience. Don't lose sight of the fact that these people are driven as much by the challenge of the work as by salary and job security. Their rewards come from doing interesting research, being published, and gaining the respect of colleagues in their field. You need to set in place mechanisms to help them to achieve these rewards. Let team members make presentations on project activities they have a major role in to the customer and the sponsor and to colleagues on other projects.

Self-Development for the Project Manager

You need to develop you own skills, too. If you have been a technical specialist, project management is probably a role for which you have had no training but to which you were assigned because of your superior technical knowledge and skill. That is the route to project manager for most people. Think back on how you regarded managers when you were an engineer, a scientist, a psychologist, or whatever, working on projects. You can expect that your former peers will regard you in the same way—as someone who has abandoned your professional career for money and is now just a bureaucrat.

If you are honest, you will have to admit that they have a point. As a project manager you will find it difficult to keep current in the state of the art in your specialty. You have a new specialty now and new responsibilities. Your focus needs to be less on technical details and more on becoming an effective manager who makes it possible for others to do good work with your support. You also should not neglect your own self-development, because in today's highly matrixed work environment, your own time may also be divided so that you are responsible for specific tasks as a team member on projects led by other project managers. As you gain project management skills, you will be a more valuable member in every assignment.

Rich Cebula confesses that he used to have a healthy disdain for management and managers when he was a project scientist. However, as he has gained more management experience, his opinion has changed. He still enjoys technical challenges, but he also enjoys the aspects of his job that relate to seeing that people are happy and are doing tasks well. He is glad that because he has made an effort to learn his staff's capabilities, he is often able to find an appropriate place for them on another project when a task is eliminated on his own project.

Self-Assessment of Project Management Skills

Prepare for your new role by doing some self-assessment. Ask yourself:

- What strengths do I have that I can build on? These may include:
  — A high level of knowledge of the technical work to be accomplished.
  — The confidence of superiors in the organization and a good track record of previous success experiences doing complex tasks on other projects.
- What are the weaknesses I need to overcome or compensate for? These might include:
  — Limited project management skills.
  — A structured, linear approach to project management.
- How can I develop the project management skills I need now? Some strategies include:
  — Going to meetings on project management, team management, time management, and communication skills

that are offered by your organization or by professional groups in your area.

— Reading the literature available from the professional groups devoted to various aspects of project management. Resources are listed in the back of this book.

— Seeking an experienced and effective project manager in your own or another organization and asking him or her to be your mentor as you gain experience in your new role.

— Developing your listening skills. Practice them with your mentor, then make them a natural part of the way you interact with your team and the project stakeholders.

• How well do I manage time and stress—my own and others'? Project management can be highly stressful. Some project staff members we interviewed for this book told of staying overnight at their desks on many occasions. One woman admitted she had not had a weekend off in months. Yet we also interviewed successful project managers who consider such work schedules entirely inappropriate, either for themselves or their team members. Some questions to address include:

— Are travel and overtime causing problems for parents and others on the team who have family responsibilities? Be sensitive to people's life situations. Not dealing with these issues risks burnout, and you may not detect it before it has affected the project. Get the team to work with you to find ways to deal with these problems. On a recent trip, we met several young people who told us that their company policy was to let the team members schedule trips out of town so that they could return on Thursday night and then work at home on Fridays. That gave them a longer weekend with their families, without taking away from and perhaps even enhancing their productivity.

— Are competing project assignments causing stress for my team members? Find out what responsibilities team members have on other projects and negotiate with the other project managers, so that people are not forced to constantly choose which of two or more different assignments they will work on—or are expected to work on full time.

When we pull an all-nighter, it's for D&D (Dungeons and Dragons). . . . We've got our priorities straight.

Nick Cotello (1996, 71)

Enter the New Hero! The Boss Who Knows You Have a Life.

—Sue Shellenbarger (1996, B-1)

Assess Your Own Ongoing Performance

Constantly assess your performance. Mary Sand advises program managers to ask themselves at critical points in a project, What went well? Why? Many large organizations have sophisticated tools and strategies to do this assessment. But even if you are a one-person project, you can list the things you did that made it go well and the things you did that caused problems. Ask yourself, Why did these problems occur? What better solutions could I have come up with? Make a list of problems and possible solutions, then keep it to refer to in later projects. If you are a first-time project manager, you should do this at the end of each day, take it out at the beginning of the next day and say, I won't make this mistake again today!

If your company has a 360-degree feedback system, take advantage of it to find out how your performance is perceived by others. Encourage everyone to get involved with the system, so that they can get useful feedback and provide useful feedback to you and to each other. Be sure that everyone on your team knows what they should do if problems arise, and be sure they are comfortable in giving you information, both good and bad, in a timely fashion—not when it is too late.

Training and Development of Project Staff

Some of the skills needed to complete project tasks have to be developed during the project, and some, like learning new software, are usually acquired quickly. But on most long-term projects, you will need to budget time and provide training to assist people in learning more complex new skills. If possible, let team members teach other; if this not possible, provide training when the skill is needed and can be immediately used. A new skill that is not practiced is lost. To ensure that you know the capabilities of the people on your project team, when you meet each week with each team member, discuss changes that are going to affect their work and find out whether they need special help to prepare for them.

Because you are likely to need people with particular skills on an ongoing basis, you should develop a database of people and skills. Share this database with the other project managers in your network. It can be a valuable resource for many projects and a benefit to the people who are listed in it. You should update this database at points in the project when people gain new skills and experience, and check with staff at the end of the project to be sure their skill list is current. We have found this type of database far more useful than a bank of résumés that are nearly always out of date.

Caution people on your project team so that they are making a well-informed choice if they decide to increase their skills in technical areas for which there is a limited market. This can result in their becoming so narrowly specialized that they will be eligible for few job openings and promotions. On the other hand, if you decide to let people take training in new skills, then provide the opportunity for them to use the skills. This can be a risk for you, because the team member who just learned the new skill—for example, a programming language—will take more time at first than a more experienced person. But you need to take a longer view and consider this an investment that will expand your team's skill set and enhance your reputation as a project manager who is committed to developing people. Having good, dependable people eager to work with you mitigates a great deal of uncertainty in managing projects.

The Project Manager as Broker of Professional Interests

On any project, there are likely to be several different kinds of professionals working on different aspects of the job, each with their own perspectives and priorities. As project manager, you will need to reconcile these perspectives to accomplish the project goals. For example: Motorola's William Wiggenhorn, Vice President for Training and Education, described the problem his company faced when it began to team up traditional electrical engineers, with their white shirts and pencil holders, with software engineers in sandals and T-shirts (1988). "Learn to love your software engineer," became a Motorola slogan because of the business need to have these two very different engineering cultures work productively together.

Besides trying to teach your various specialists to work with each other, you should also encourage team members to learn something about each other's disciplines. Allow members of the project team the time to participate, both as members and presenters, at some of the many professional association–sponsored workshops, conferences, and meetings that are offered in their disciplines. Use these occasions as opportunities for sharing new information with the rest of the team. Let individuals get the recognition they deserve for their professional expertise. Help the team to use and appreciate that expertise and take pride in its positive impact on the project. If different specialties can't seem to speak the same language, it is sometimes helpful to have an expert on group dynamics show them how to develop an understanding of their different viewpoints and learn to work together.

Staff Development as a Three-Way Responsibility

Make it clear that although you will facilitate their efforts to the extent that you can, in the final analysis, team members have to take responsibility for their own development. Present staff development as a three-level process. You can take sole responsibility to arrange for some development activities; you can take joint responsibility for some; and for some, they must take sole responsibility. For example:

- You can make job assignments that offer development opportunities.
- You can support such self-development activities as brown bag lunches in which staff members share new information; but team members must take the initiative to attend on their own time.
- But the most important self-development activities are those for which the team as a whole and each team member take individual responsibility—seeking information from each other and learning new skills from other team members on the job and learning from external sources like professional meetings and publications.

Make it clear that you welcome their efforts to expand their capabilities and will recognize them in making assignments and in official performance appraisals.

Managing Virtual Projects

Virtual Team Training and Self-Development

Team training and development are critical in managing any project, but they are especially critical in managing virtual project teams and organizations. Lori's company is a virtual company, made up of many people who have their own businesses or who are freelance consultants to a variety of companies. She also serves as a project team member with some of her colleagues' companies.

In this loose confederation, people maintain their own identities but work together on a semiregular basis as members of each others' organizations and project teams. Many confederation members meet regularly to participate in staff development training. Some training sessions cover project team skills, such as using CompuServe to send e-mail and project work files to each other and to clients. Others are conducted at professional meetings and conferences to update professional skills and knowledge, with members of the confederation attending as both participants and presenters.

These professional forums are extremely valuable to people who are isolated either by the pressures of work or by distance. They provide a good opportunity to meet some of the social needs of a project team, while providing a stimulating way to learn new skills. For example, as of this writing, most of the members of our virtual confederation are either current or past board members for one or more professional associations.

Your virtual project teams may not want to get this involved, but we definitely recommend that they participate in regular self-development efforts, whether they do it together or as individuals. We have found that a major reason we continue to enjoy working together is our common drive to learn how to do things better, which gives us new insights to bring to our project design meetings and new ideas to present to our clients.

Virtual Team Work Processes

Mary Sand of the FAA often works on projects in which team members are at FAA regional offices around the country, and she has developed a system for working with project staff at different locations. At the beginning of a project, she sets the stage by calling each person individually, introducing herself, and discussing the project with them. Then she sends out discussion questions to everyone and schedules a teleconference with the entire group. They use their responses to the questions to explore in the teleconference how they can best work together in the most economical and efficient way. Faxes, on-screen conferencing, and teleconferences are all possibilities. They discuss the times, sites, and constraints involved in each of these methods.

Rick Mathews and his coauthors, writing in *Performance & Instruction* (1996) said their virtual project team found that time zone disparities and conflicting commitments made teleconferencing impractical at first. They had to create a table of members' telephone numbers and e-mail data, with times converted to a common standard; and then assign one team member to notify all the others in advance that there would be a teleconference. Before they could make good use of e-mail, they also had to test the e-mail capabilities at each team member's site, to see what text and graphics they could send and receive. Although they did not have groupware available, this is also a good option for sharing work among dispersed sites.

Jackie Dobrovolny, Tim Spannaus, and Lori in their presentation about "Managing the Virtual Project" (1996) found that many of their session participants agreed that a critical element to success is installing and using a common technology architecture. However, they also found that they could not forget to train all of the team members on the appropriate use of the technology. For example, Tim learned to his chagrin that the listserve (electronic conference site) set up for his project involving people in Germany, England, Detroit, Flint, and Denver, was rarely used as it was intended—that is, as a shared space to review interim project products and to discuss project issues for ongoing project feedback. Without that feedback link, he ran into several situations that could have been diffused if the team had dealt with them earlier, when they arose.

Just as we said in chapter 3, the agreements and understandings made in the commitment stage are important to the overall success of any project. With virtual teams, you will probably have to do even more to establish the common working ground and skills needed by all the team members.

Ongoing Human Resource Management

Dealing with Conflict and Frustration

Good project managers listen, coach, encourage feedback, value openness, and admit emotions. They manage conflict, rather than ignore or disallow it. Karen Taylor described a frustrating experience that an ELF team had. They had spent long hours to prepare a proposal and did not win the contract. To let everyone vent their frustrations, the project manager took the team to a brick oven restaurant with an open fire, and everyone cast into the flames the section of the luckless proposal they had developed. You won't always be able to be this dramatic, but you should recognize when people are feeling frustrated and angry about work assignments and give them an avenue to put the bad experience behind them.

Fostering a good working relationship among the project team members is an excellent buffer against risk and uncertainty. By contrast, a project where there is conflict wastes time and energy that could be spent on productive activity. Working with people who are not enthusiastic and who resent the time they have to spend on the project is demoralizing to other staff. Find out what is causing their lack of enthusiasm. You may not have a solution to their problem, but you can suggest a starting point toward a solution. Often, conflicts on teams are the result of long-established grudges that did not begin with this team but are affecting its performance. Let the team members involved know as soon as you identify such a problem that their conflict is adversely affecting team performance. Give each person a chance to describe his or her point of view; take no sides but insist that they agree on a solution so that the project will not suffer from their disagreement. Then set up a second meeting to be sure the situation is improving.

Problems become more serious as a project goes along. Try to deal with them up front. Set down guidelines and quality standards at the outset. Wherever possible, provide templates to facilitate consistency. Making people guess what you want can lead to high levels of frustration for everyone.

Concentrate everyone's efforts on being sure that the first phase of the project is well done before starting a second phase. Identifying and solving problems early in the project give people confidence that they know what you expect, and that they can meet your quality levels. This reduces the risk of conflict and frustration; however, if the early project products are barely satisfactory, a precedent is set, and later phases will suffer.

Take Action to Improve Performance

Ron Koroscil of Pitney Bowes Manufacturing Maintenance says he sets ground rules and makes sure that everybody on the team knows them. If people don't follow the rules, he meets with whoever is out of compliance and points out what they are doing or not doing. He tells them, Your performance is hurting the team. What do we need to do to help you improve? Then together they make a plan for improving the performance, and he monitors the progress and provides feedback on a regular basis to the team member. He makes it clear that his expectation is that the team member can and will improve.

Make it clear that you want and expect consistent performance. If the goal is to have 20 items completed each day, some people will equate that with 100 a week. But it is not the same. One team member's irregular daily output makes it impossible for other people to meet their output goals.

You need to assess the personalities of the people on your project team to determine how you can motivate each person to deliver the best possible performance. Some people are eager for advancement and welcome tasks that give them opportunities to show their skill and dedication. Other equally good workers do not want to take on high-pressure assignments. But don't confuse eagerness to do difficult work and be promoted with the ability to actually perform! Persuading a less ambitious but more competent team member to take on a challenging task may result in a better performance than would have been achieved by a team member who is more concerned with a promotion than with doing the difficult task required.

Delegate Appropriately

As project manager, you must control the project as it goes along. You should manage in a collaborative manner but don't delegate to others decisions for which you are responsible. Avoid the temptation to delegate just because you are too busy, or not very interested in a particular aspect of the project. If you do this, you can easily lose sight of what's going on. The project can take a wrong turn and you won't know it. Does this mean that you should not delegate? Of course not, but you will be responsible to your client for the decisions others make—so delegate wisely and be sure you know what is being done. Get briefings on the outcomes of tasks you have delegated before the work proceeds to the next task.

Provide Clear Direction

When you review the work of your team members, provide professional direction. Give useful feedback that will result in a better product. Don't say, This is terrible! Explain why it is unacceptable. Say, This does not hit the mark—it doesn't get across the message we discussed. Revise it to make sure that message is conveyed, and let me see it again. Resist the impulse to redo the work yourself.

The GAO gives this advice to managers reviewing document drafts:

- Tell the author what you like about their work.
- Match your feedback to the product. Don't waste a lot of time on early drafts or prototypes, just provide encouragement at this stage.
- Be specific and clear in your feedback.
- Distinguish substance from personal preference. The goal is to improve the product, not make it read as though you did it.
- Offer fixes to help solve the problems. Often people know they have a problem, but they need help to fix it.
- Use automated feedback to comment on written products (e.g., redline, strikeout, underline, document compare, and comment).
- Use the LAN to avoid commenting on out-of-date drafts.

Mary Sand of the FAA warns that project managers should never be authoritarian but should be available to everyone, because you never know who may offer a good idea. But don't let people take up a lot of your time discussing ideas that have already been rejected. Tell them the idea was already considered, without discouraging them from bringing new ideas.

Summary

You have taken on a big job, that of leader, appraiser, motivator, developer, counselor, coach, encourager, prodder, cheerleader, friend—a seemingly impossible task. The risk to you and your project is that you do not recognize that this task is important, possibly neglecting these issues while concentrating on the project tasks. We and our colleagues have overwhelmingly found that a key element to the success of a project is how the project team operates, both as individuals and as a team. How well you deal with the team members' skills, knowledge, attitudes, concerns, fears, and styles will determine how successful you are as a project manager. We encourage you to learn, study, grow—to become a better human resource manager. Your project sponsors, clients, and teams will thank you for it.

Chapter 6

The Project Manager as Communicator and Change Agent

Guiding and supporting change projects that introduce new technologies and systems into organizations to increase effectiveness and efficiency are becoming more difficult, and less certain of success (Caldwell 1994). As technologies evolve and organizations adapt to take advantage of the efficiencies in work processes that technology makes possible, unanticipated outcomes can inhibit the expected benefits. These include schedule delays, multiple redesigns of the new technologies, and anxious, angry workers who resist adapting to the changes.

Reengineering projects (Andrews and Stalick 1994) typically apply the sociotechnical engineering model principles, which call for integrating the human, work, and technology systems of an organization into a new paradigm for work performance (Block, Petrella, and Weisbord 1992). Such projects find themselves dealing with many uncertainties, which seem to compound themselves in more complex projects.

As project manager, you will often need to help your customer cope with the changes your project is intended to bring about. In this chapter, we discuss the types of communication that are essential and the special risks inherent in the role of the project manager as change agent.

Project Management and the Change Model

Only individuals can decide to change and only individuals can actually change.

—Clay Carr (1996, 182)

Many projects involve activities and outcomes that are intended to result in changes that threaten long-established ways of doing business. Projects that involve business process reengineering, team building, downsizing, or rightsizing face the risk that stakeholders who find the change threatening may sabotage the project and cause it to fail. New information technology projects may integrate work processes that formerly were disconnected, each in its own "stovepipe" with its own staff, budget, and responsibilities. Integration of work processes often results in job redesign that combines previously separate functions and reduces management levels and staffing, a change that is usually unwelcome to the affected people, particularly as it breaks up relationships among workers and between workers and supervisors. People at all levels fear becoming redundant—a legitimate fear!

Change Models—Old and New

Most traditional change models such as the one shown in Figure 6-1 (Beckhard and Harris 1977 and Farrell and Broude 1987) show movement from a current state or old system, through a transition state or middle ground, to a new system or future state of equilibrium. Change process models, when they integrate human system change with technology and work systems changes, recommend using the change process states to create new systems to direct the new activities needed by the redesigned or reengineered work processes (Bancroft 1992). The change effort is focused on creating

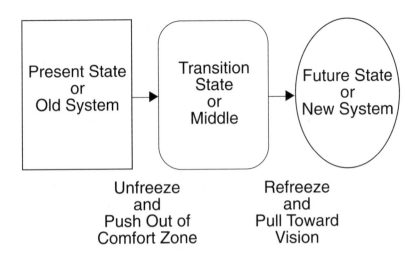

Figure 6-1. Change Model

the new status quo by directing, tracking, and recording all the activities and people involved in the change process.

In effect, most change models used in systems development and organizational reengineering efforts share a Newtonian image of the universe. This view assumes that we can manage by breaking the change process into its parts, defining the parts and the interactions among the parts, and objectively measuring the system input and output for each part. This model assumes that the better we can objectively measure things in our world, the better able we will be to predict precise results.

It reflects a belief in an orderly Newtonian universe, in which atoms and planets move in predictable ways, and new information can be fit into existing structures. Similarly, a chart that depicts the hierarchy in an organization shows that the person in each box is responsible, directly or indirectly, to those in the boxes above; and the person in the top box oversees all the others—the buck stops there. If a new function must be integrated into the organization, the change becomes a new box added to the chart. Everything else stays the same.

A different and, we believe, more accurate way of looking at managing change is suggested by Margaret Wheatley. In her book *Leadership and the New Science* (1992), she suggests adopting the core principle of quantum physics: That there is no objective reality; there is only what we create through our interaction with others and with events. Thus, the basic premise of quantum physics is that nothing is predictable. Everything changes and adapts as new information is integrated. Observation and interaction create the new reality. This sounds more like the model of most our projects; how about yours?

So, while we generally accept the idea that change is about moving people from a current state, through a transition state, and to a future state, we also accept that there is no one path to take that will work for all our project stakeholders. In addition, we know our stakeholders will be influenced and redirected by their interactions with others going through the change process. This leads us back to trying to manage the change process by concentrating on each person involved in the change at the same time we're dealing with the overall change within the organization. Yes, this does resemble trying to pat your head and rub your stomach at the same time, an awkward and difficult thing to do, especially for those of us who are not very physically dexterous. Yet the ultimate success of any project hinges on how it is perceived by those affected, directly or indirectly. If they see it as a positive process, chances are they will like the results. If they aren't brought through the change states successfully, they most likely will hate the results.

Change Agentry

If the success of your project depends on the acceptance of major change, and chances are it will, you need to be especially conscious of your role as a change agent. We suggest you start by looking at each of your stakeholder groups to see how ready and capable they are for this change. Diane

Dormant has developed a comprehensive process (Change Mapping^{SM}) for providing change agents with the tools to foster acceptance of a change. Central to that process are the five stages individuals go through to reach the desired future state (Dormant, 1992, 179):

- Awareness. The person knows something about the change, has heard it mentioned and explained, but usually has little opinion about the project change itself or denies that it will affect him or her.
- Curiosity. The person asks questions or expresses concern about the effect of change on him or herself, often exhibiting signs of denial, resistance, and defensive retreat.
- Visualization. The person actively asks questions to understand the relationship and effect of the change to him or herself and the organization.
- Learning. The person participates in learning how to use or implement the change and has opinions and concerns about the quality and design of the change.
- Use. The person actively uses and integrates change into daily work and can describe and explain the change to others.

Figure 6-2 shows an adopter's path through the different states along a timeline. Don't be fooled; this is not a one-way journey. Although the research on change and individuals concludes that all change adopters usually go through all these stages in order, it also shows that adopters differ in their rates of adoption, and most important to you as the project manager, they may reject change and revert to a previous stage at any time. This means that you will not be able to force your stakeholders to a later stage of change until you have dealt with the earlier ones. Furthermore, it means that activities to help the stakeholders through the change will need to be done multiple times, to catch all the people coming through the various stages for the first time and to snag those who have retreated backward.

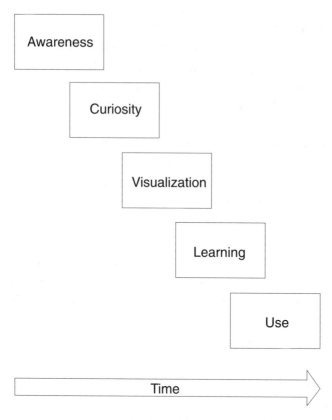

Figure 6-2. Change Adopter Stages (Dormant 1992)

Change Agent Strategies

In your project manager as change agent role, you need to be aware of which of these change stages your stakeholders are in, because you must facilitate the stakeholders' movement from the awareness stage to the adoption of the change stage.

Diane Dormant provides some suggestions about appropriate strategies for helping stakeholders throughout the change (1992, 179). Table 6-1, based on Dormant's model, lists an approach to use for each change stage with some specific suggestions from us and from Farrell and Broude (1987) about techniques. Activities that are appropriate for your particular project and stakeholder group can easily be identified by you and your project team based on these suggestions—for example, video briefings to introduce change, FAQs (frequently asked questions) to inform, demonstrations to show, workshops to train, help desks to support. We recommend you include activities for dealing with all the stages of change directly on your project work plan. And don't forget that you have to do these activities multiple times throughout the project, to catch the stragglers and reverters. A typical miscalculation that we have seen is the assumption that one announcement meeting, one question-and-answer session, one demonstration, one field test, and one final rollout event are all that are needed to handle the change part of a project. This approach only catches the small percentage of people that were predisposed to go along with the change in the first place. It won't help you bring along all the other affected stakeholders who might need more time and repeated examples before they become committed to the change.

Table 6-1. Change Agent Strategies

If the stakeholder is in this stage of adoption . . .	The appropriate strategy to use is:
Awareness	Introduce • Advertise change • Point out positives • Link to meeting needs and eliminating dissatisfactions
Curiosity	Inform • Provide clear, concise explanations • Answer questions • Elicit concerns, acknowledge difficulties • Present viable approach to change
Visualization	Show • Demonstrate change • Conduct user testing and reviews
Learning	Train • Conduct workshops • Provide job aids and quick reference guides
Use	Support • Provide technical assistance • Provide reference documentation

We tend to think in terms of chants: Once is not enough and Each one reach one. The first saying helps us remember the need to repeat these activities through the project. The second phrase helps us select change process activities that continually incorporate more people, who then become change agents for others. This incorporation process can be facilitated through the networks you have identified and established, as we discussed in chapter 4.

Identifying and Dealing with Adopter Stages

At the start of the project, some stakeholders will be ready to adopt the change. These people probably are the project sponsors. Rather than fearing change, they look forward to the improvements it will bring. They will be well into the visualization stage. Because they are the project sponsors, you may get the impression at the outset that they are representative of all the stakeholders. However, trust us, as you spend more time with the other stakeholder groups, you will find that some are still at the awareness stage, and others are just beginning to recognize how the project outcomes may affect them.

Early in the project, meet with the stakeholders and discuss the change and why it is needed. Get reactions to the anticipated change, and clear up any misunderstandings. Acknowledge people's objections to the changes. Don't be apologetic, but instead ask for suggestions as to how these objections can be overcome. Solicit the group's support for the change and promise to keep everyone informed as the project progresses.

In this and later contacts, try to continually assess the degree of acceptance of the change among the stakeholder group. Stakeholders who oppose the changes may not directly admit it, but as Susan Stalick of Business Reengineering Resources, Inc., pointed out in a recent ISPI Conference

(1996) presentation, they can use many methods to demonstrate their resistance to the change and to impede it. The evidence that change can be thwarted is found in the statistics that show most reengineering efforts have failed.

Dormant and others involved in implementing change (Farrell and Broude 1987 and Fossum 1989) recommend watching people's behavior and noting what is said. These expressions can then be placed or posted in a chart of the stages of change, showing you where these stakeholders are in the change process. For example, if the bulk of the expressions (e.g., What's going to happen to my job? or Why does our department have to do this? We always get the raw end of the deal, or even What do I get out of this?) end up in the curiosity part of the chart, you need to figure out ways to help people identify, understand, and deal with those concerns.

The late Clay Carr pointed out that what we call organizational change is ". . . the sum total of changes decided upon and made by the individuals . . ." and individuals can subvert the process at any stage. Duck (1993) says that for change to occur in an organization, every individual must think, feel or do something different; a challenging goal for any project.

Ron Koroscil and Jack D'Urso of Pitney Bowes, in describing the acceptance of change in their manufacturing group, said that people divided into three groups: those on each side of the fence and those on the fence. Their advice was to concentrate on encouraging those already on the change side, because when they receive encouragement and support, they influence the fence sitters to accept the change. Finally the change acceptors reach a critical mass; and those on the other side of the fence see the inevitability of the change and accept it, too (1996). Dormant likewise suggests concentrating effort on the early adopters who are also opinion leaders, because they can influence many others in the organization. Your networks should be able to help you identify who these people are. If possible, get them on your team. If not possible, provide them with the material that can let them help others informally. This will definitely help get the majority of the stakeholders over the fence in time to allow the successful implementation of the change.

A Change Project Example

For example, let's consider a project that was described to us. An elected official was receiving complaints from constituents that response to citizen letters was too slow. The official discussed the problem with the county information systems staff and they recommended improving the workflow by introducing imaging technology and a local area network. By using this system, mail could be scanned on arrival and directed immediately to the on-line mailbox of the appropriate staff person to answer it. Other relevant correspondence could be easily retrieved, and the time to prepare a response would be greatly reduced.

The official was delighted. Technology now existed to help her to meet her constituents' needs quickly. She was already at the adoption or use stage. However, no one in her office was even at the awareness stage! As they became aware of the planned changes, they had many reservations. Would the scanners be reliable? Some people had had bad experiences with early versions. Mailroom clerks who had always read the mail and routed to the proper persons feared that their jobs would be eliminated—they were in a stage of curiosity, expressing concern for their jobs and work. Correspondence clerks were interested in seeing how the imaging system would translate the paper copy they were used to into screen displays. They were at the visualization stage. Some of them had gone to a trade show to get some experience with a similar system. They were at the learning stage. So in this one office, all stages of change were present, and the official would need to employ all the appropriate change strategies.

The official needed to back up a bit and get everyone on the same wavelength. After she assigned and briefed a project team that included representatives of all the stakeholder groups, she scheduled an all-hands meeting to announce the project and entertain questions and answers about it. (Introduce/Inform). People were encouraged to visit her or any member of the project team privately to discuss the project and how it would affect them individually (Inform). Demos of the technology were scheduled several times over the next few months to make sure everyone got to see it in action (Inform/Show). Newsletters and e-mail announcements were distributed to keep everyone informed about the project's process and describe some of the system features (Introduce/Show). At each regular staff meeting she took time for an update and questions on the project (Introduce/ Inform). Pilot tests of the system were run in each department to see how the system needed to be modified to work (Train), and a representative from each department was trained in how to train others in their department to use the system (Train/Support). Finally the installation of the system was completed and celebrated at an all-hands meeting.

This is a small example of how you, as a project manager in today's work environments, will need to respond to stakeholders at all of these stages in your projects and how you can tailor your interactions to be appropriate for the stage the people are in.

Develop a Plan to Introduce the Changes

Early in the project, you need to develop a communication plan that will ensure that every stakeholder becomes aware of the changes your project will create. This plan can include helping the client organization to design posters or hold meetings to advertise the positive changes that are expected. For example, in the county correspondence project, this plan would focus on explaining how the technology will simplify the work, thus providing a way to be more responsive to the public and improve the electoral chances of the boss.

From the description of the project outcomes, try to envision what self-concerns people might have. We find that they are usually worried about job loss and about whether they will be able to handle their new roles. Typically, they also worry about whether their experience will translate to the new work environment. As a project manager, you can't afford to ignore these concerns; if you don't put them to rest, their worries can derail your project. You need to provide a forum in which such concerns can be expressed and where people can get reliable information from people they trust.

Some people will be at the visualization stage. These are likely to be those who are most frustrated with the current system and ready to explore ways to improve it. For them, the communication plan should provide examples of successful uses of the technology in similar settings.

If there are stakeholders who are ready for a demonstration, involve them as early as possible in testing prototypes. Until prototypes are ready, you can suggest providing opportunities to attend demonstrations or visit sites where they can try out a similar system. While the new system is being developed, these people also can begin to learn the skill sets they will need. For example, these people can attend short courses in any new software that will be used in the system.

Include adequate time for hand-holding after people have adopted the changes. In situations like the mail response example, there are likely to be many discouraging moments when people will begin pining for the good old days. Don't ignore this tendency—if this thinking is not challenged, your project can fail, as people lose confidence in the benefits of change and begin to subvert it. Remind them about how the good old days weren't always so good. Help them put the old pictures away and begin focusing on the picture of the new world.

Even if you are new at project management, you will find that most projects do represent some level of change, to at least some stakeholders. Extensive discussion of change management is beyond the scope of this book, but we want to stimulate and encourage your interest in learning about facilitating change, because if you fail to do this in a project that is focused on major change, you will be inviting failure.

Chapter 7

Managing Risk Throughout the Project

You will never eliminate risk and uncertainty in project management—that is the major premise of this book. But, you can cope with them more effectively by becoming more consciously aware of the types of interactions and circumstances that create uncertainty. The risks at each project stage are different, but they are always there. In Table 7-1 we have listed some of the questions we ask to identify uncertainty and risk. If you answer these questions with Nos, you are probably endangering the potential success of the project. Think about these as the warning signs of danger, and take action to resolve the problem. In this chapter we will highlight some of the ways you will have to deal with these and areas of uncertainty throughout your projects.

Opportunity Stage Risks

Risk assessment should begin at the opportunity stage as soon as the potential project is first identified. All the project managers we interviewed agree that the biggest project management challenge is to get it right at the front end. Our version of getting it right means correctly answering the questions:

- Is this the right opportunity?

- Have we correctly defined it?
- Is this the right client?

Table 7-1. Project Risk Assessment Questions

Stage	Questions
Throughout the project life cycle	• Is this project still a priority business need (or does it still contribute to meeting a priority business need)? • Does this project (or its activities or products) still satisfy the stakeholders' goals? • Is the technology being used or specified still available and appropriate for the project process or solution? • Are there any new or different competitive or environmental factors that will impact the project's activities or outcomes?
Opportunity	• Is this still the right opportunity or problem to solve? • Have we correctly and completely defined and analyzed the problem or opportunity? • Is this the right client? • Have we clearly defined the project goal, objectives, and critical success factors? • Have we identified the areas of uncertainty and risk associated with this project?
Commitment	• Have we defined the right tasks? • Have we secured the right resources? • Does the project team have the right competencies? • Are we using the right technology? • Can we produce quality products within the time and budget agreed to?
Implementation	• Is this still the right thing to do? • Is this (project process or outputs) what we set out to do? Are we achieving our critical success factors? • Does what we are doing still fit within the project goals and objectives? • Is the project process within the time and budget plans? • Are the resources performing as expected? • Is the technology performing as required and expected?
Conclusion	• Will we know when we are done? How? • Are the project products distributed to the customers? • Has the project team transferred the documentation and materials required to the operational areas? • Has the project team completed all its assigned project work and been reassigned to other work?

If the answer to these questions is Yes, then the project is more likely to follow a predictable pattern. The risk that the project will not succeed is high if the answers to these questions are ambiguous.

Assessing Whether This Is the Right Project

Failure later in the execution of a project usually results from failure to do the front-end work right at the opportunity stage. This is a major concern for managers in every size and type of organization. If you are a beginner in project management, the challenge to get business is especially keen and can easily lead you to make poor judgments about risk that would be apparent to a more experienced project manager. When you are anxious to get the job, you are less likely to apply the necessary discipline to assess the risk objectively.

A focus group of experienced project managers at a May 1996 ISPI Workshop, which Mary facilitated with Amy Titus (DeWeaver and Titus), identified these common mistakes that project managers make in assessing whether an opportunity is right:

- Taking an overly optimistic view and refusing to recognize problems, especially in projects involving technology.
- Making a decision to proceed with a project, based on incomplete or incorrect information.
- Failing to ensure that upper management will support the project.
- Overlooking a lack of commitment by those who should be stakeholders, which is rooted in their unsatisfactory experiences with similar past projects.

Correctly Defining the Project

Failure to correctly define a project is a common cause of project failure. At the opportunity stage, you need to make accurate judgments about the customer's objective for the project. What was the real impetus for the project? Is there data to support the need for the project, and is the need critical enough to ensure that the project will have support through its completion? Projects that are considered urgent at the outset often are later seen as not valued and are abandoned.

In the hypothetical case of the Dinner Out project in chapter 2, the project lost support of management when the competitive environment changed. If your project is in midstream when this happens, you can experience severe cash flow problems, and your project team members are likely to be faced with both professional and financial insecurity. If you think it is likely that support for the project will weaken, either reject the opportunity, or propose to organize the work in discrete phases, with payments tied to phase completion and with opportunities to rescope the project objectives at the start of each new phase.

Don't expect that the statement of work provided in the customer's request for proposals necessarily represents all of the anticipated project outcomes. Before you commit to developing a proposal, review these carefully with a client representative if they appear ambiguous. Then, in discussions before the start of the project, review them again to see whether the scope or requirements have changed.

You also need to carefully define the products and services the customer expects to be produced. Then assess your expertise and the resources available to you to be sure you can produce these outcomes. It is usually a mistake to undertake a project, however much encouragement you are given to do so, if it is really outside the area of your expertise, unless the customer is aware of and agrees to pay for the learning curve you and your team will require to reach proficiency. Even in this circumstance, you are likely to encounter frustration and discouragement as you attempt to reach proficiency within the time allotted. On the other hand, if the project requirements would be equally new for your competitors, this type of project challenge can provide a welcome chance to broaden your expertise for this and future projects, and a successful project outcome is likely to ensure follow-on work with this customer.

Although as a project manager you are not expected to be a contract expert, you should also know what type of contract the customer is offering. Whether you are working independently or within an organization, you will be expected to tailor your project work to fit the cash flow the project generates. If the payment schedule proposed is not likely to cover your project costs and meet your organization's profit goals throughout the life of the project, it is probably not an appropriate project unless you can negotiate changes.

Assessing Whether This Is the Right Client

For a project to succeed, there needs to be a fit between the project and the potential customer. Project manager, project team, and customer should have a collaborative relationship. However, many times a customer takes an adversarial attitude toward the project. This may be based on previous unfortunate experiences with other projects, or it may be because this attitude has served this particular customer well in another context. For example, if the customer has had a successful career in litigious situations, where there are winners and losers, he or she will deal with your project as a win-lose proposition and you will not be able to establish the level of trust needed to work collaboratively.

Accepting a project when there is this type of clash of styles will return to haunt you at the implementation stage. Your project can founder and even fail because you cannot reach agreement on how to deal with the need to modify the original accepted plan, which as we have said previously, is inevitable given the uncertainties that surround the typical project at every stage.

To assess whether the project is a good match for their firm, at the opportunity, or as they call it, the project scoping stage, Anderson Consulting asks questions like these about the potential client:

- Is their organization stable?
- Would we be working with a sponsor at a high enough level in the organization to provide the necessary support for the project?
- Will our involvement be a large enough part of the total effort so that we can control what we will be doing, or do we risk being accountable without having control of the project?

They then assess what internal resources would be required to pursue the opportunity: What would it take to prepare a proposal? How big is the effort? Is this potentially what they call a "Tier I" client—one with whom Anderson Consulting can develop a long-term relationship?

Commitment Stage Risks

At the commitment stage, you decide that the project and the client are right, and you have, or can get, the resources to do the project work. This usually means you must develop a proposal describing what you will do and how, what resources you will need, and what everything will cost. You then present this proposal to the potential sponsors. There are lots of risks involved here.

Time Estimates

It is relatively easy to estimate the time it will take to do routine tasks with which you've had extensive experience. But Rich Cebula of Hughes STX points out that when a project involves a new task, for example, trying to characterize instrument performance on a satellite, it is difficult to estimate how long it will take. The project team may propose to do the assessment in six weeks, but the vagaries of the instrument's performance can cause it to behave in an unexpected manner, causing the task to take eight weeks. Uncertainties like this pose risks to project budgets and staffing requirements.

Cebula says, in his experience, this kind of uncertainty is inevitable. We agree. You should make the best estimates possible, and then explain in your proposal that there is some uncertainty in the estimates, and why. Once the project starts, you need to keep the customer informed of the status of the effort, tell them about any problems being encountered, and be ready to offer possible solutions. For example, a team might get 90 percent of the data they need in three weeks, but then estimate that it will take five weeks to get the rest of the data, rather than an additional three weeks. Cebula then must decide with the client how to solve the additional time problem. Is it necessary to spend two additional weeks to get the other 10 percent, especially if it requires reallocating people and taking them off other projects? Is 90 percent enough? Are there alternative ways to get the remaining data? Can people double up—do two jobs? (This is not usually feasible, because people tend to be overallocated already.) Can the task be postponed from June until August, when people will be more available?

Estimating requires continuous juggling of the three main elements involved in project management: budgeted time, cost, and quality (i.e., fast, cheap, and good mentioned in chapter 3). The old saw has it that you can only get two out of three in any project. We feel that you can get all three sometimes, but you can't hold all three constant for the duration of the project. The most you can have constant at any one time is two of the elements. That means that you and your client will have to assess progress regularly against the stated estimates and make adjustments when needed.

Changing Goals

David Meyers of HTI says he views the original project plan as a stimulus—a starting point. A project manager must treat the project as an organic entity that needs to grow and change as new stimuli appear. Meyers knows most clients want to see goals and timetables, and he always provides them at the start of a project. "But," he cautions, "you must continually reevaluate them as the project goes along, asking:

- Are these goals still achievable? Should they be modified based on reality?
- Are they politically feasible? Is this still what the client wants done?
- Is this client insecure about how the project is going? How can I provide reassurance?"

Mary Sand of the Federal Aviation Administration says that in her experience the greatest risk in project management is to fail to have, and to communicate, clearly outlined goals for a project and a method for moving toward the final results. This does not mean that upper management or circumstances will not require a change in direction. But you can handle that better if you had defined the original goal.

Often, she says, the project manager has a good idea of what should be done, but the client's upper management has a different idea. Equally often, the client changes direction without informing the project manager. The most carefully thought out plan will not survive if upper management changes course; but if you follow the model we discussed earlier in this book—complete the project in small increments, develop successive prototypes, and have each approved in turn—the entire project effort is not so likely to be at risk if upper management changes direction.

Sand suggests that a project manager can sometimes use a client's request for major changes after a project is under way as an opportunity to rethink the project. If you consider carefully why the client wants to make the changes, you often will be able to suggest a completely new approach that takes advantage of the experience so far with the project and that suits the client's current desires better than the original plan. For example, new software may have become available that can now be incorporated into a design change.

Getting Agreement and Commitment

Writing a proposal or commitment memo does not end the risk assessment within the commitment stage. Other experts and customers who have had no involvement with the project so far now get their chance to review the proposal and the estimates. They can recommend changes, or even cancellation of the effort, if they don't understand or agree with the ideas in the proposal. You need to use the information and analysis developed during the opportunity stage to help justify and define your project assumptions. If you still do not get commitments, you will have to return to the opportunity stage activities and refine your analysis and recommendations until you can define a project for which you can get agreement and commitments.

Establishing Outcomes and Measures

At this point in the project, if you haven't done it already, you should define all the parameters, or critical success factors (CSFs), that will be used later to determine project success, both for you and your client. Completing the project on time, within budget, and meeting specified quality levels are usually important development goals for both you and the client. You will most likely also have goals related to the specific design of the project product. For example, reduce the size of electronic storage space needed for the local network, or develop the prototype in systematic fashion to be able to identify problems and their solutions in achieving the project vision. You should also have other goals related to project outcomes. These can include such things as achieving savings in overhead and labor costs by workflow improvements, accelerating cash flow by reducing task turnaround time and early deliverables submission, or improving health and accident statistics through employee safety and wellness programs. Critical success factors and their measures are key to the overall assessment of project success. Not having them clearly defined and agreed to leaves you open to criticism and second-guessing from all sides, no matter what you do in the project.

Implementation Stage Risks

The question that you should keep uppermost in your mind throughout the implementation spirals is, Is this still the right thing to do? Any hesitation on your part to answer Yes should be a clear warning to examine the risks of proceeding without some modification. As we stated in chapter 2, organizations usually find their risks in one of four forces: business needs, stakeholders, technology, or competition and the external environment. Other factors also come into play as the project moves through the various activities planned for the implementation stage.

Risk and Changing Expectations

As the project continues into the implementation stage, where project work is done, risk management involves keeping the client aware of project progress and managing the client's expectations. At this stage it is critical that the client understands what the project scope allows. For example, the client may need to be told, This is the budget. We have to be satisfied with the outcome that this money can provide. It could be better, but the budget determines what we can do.

You should have a similar speech ready for explaining the effect of time deadlines on the budget and quality of the project products. For example, in the case of a project that is providing assistance in managing a merger and acquisition, there are legal deadlines that must be met to get the new organization into operation, and there may be time only to do what is minimally required.

Scope creep is a dreaded phenomenon by virtually all project team participants. Client expectations must be adjusted to all the project realities. While we have been encouraging you to make adjustments throughout the project based on the realities of the moment, at the same time, as a project manager, you should be conscious of the analysis and reasoning that went into the decision to start the project in the first place. If you have done your work adequately in the opportunity and commitment stages, you shouldn't have to totally redo all of your plans. Further, when the new ideas that should be incorporated come up, they should be itemized and recognized for what they are—that is, not part of the original plan but new design ideas that need to be added to the project scope. The risk is always maintaining the balance of expectations—yours, to continue the project as planned, and the customer's, to do whatever it takes to get the right result.

One major thing we recommend to help you keep track of decisions that may influence the scope and progress of project products: Keep records of decisions made in important meetings. It is easy for people to "remember" things later that were not said at all but that meet someone"s individual agenda. In fact, if a decision is made during a meeting that does impact the project effort, we tend not only to write it up, but also to circulate it to all the project stakeholders. This ensures that everyone knows about all decisions as they are made and gives them the opportunity to deal with it immediately if they feel they need to.

Risk and Project Longevity

Project managers we interviewed confirmed our own experience that if a project lasts longer than a year, there are certain to be changes in the client organization, and these changes almost always represent uncertainty and risk. New decision makers who take over ongoing projects may be unfamiliar with each specific project or may have reservations about project goals. Newcomers usually like to start something new; they have little enthusiasm for projects that were initiated by their predecessors. They often want to scale back ongoing projects or redirect them to free up funds for other projects of greater interest to them; or they may redirect the project so that work already accepted will have to be redone.

Risk Related to Change in the Sponsor

Changes in the customer's organization can put a project at special risk if the project is only very loosely linked to the organization and its overall needs. As project manager you need to develop linkages early that will expand the constituency for your project. If you fail to make the need for the project understood, it will be at grave risk as stakeholders and priorities change. To minimize this risk, be alert to changes in the client organization that can affect your project. External contractors must resist the temptation to become involved in the internal politics of the customer's organization but assess the potential impact of possible changes and stay alert to how these may affect the project. Who's in or out of favor in the client organization can have major consequences for your project. Internal project managers should also try to stay out of the politics of the internal customer's area. Keep your focus on the project objectives and relate to everyone in a friendly but professional manner. Even though you are in the same organization, you need to position yourself as an objective outsider. This is a legitimate and useful role, and it is what is expected of you. You can use this role to help the internal organization focus on what is important related to the project.

Whether internal or external, the role of an objective outsider sometimes allows you to serve as a conduit for a group's wider concerns, because of the access you have as project manager. This is a good way to build up networks and support in an organization but can backfire if you are seen as a puller of strings, or as an opportunistic meddler. Be careful to balance the need to communicate important information to those who can make decisions with the need to keep personal confidences private. Make sure that you maintain positive communications with all of the affected groups, so that any change in project sponsorship does not affect the project.

These changes may, of course, be positive for you, particularly if you are an outside contractor working on the project. For example, downsizing or other organizational changes may result in outsourcing work. If you know about these changes, you can make certain that your experience in the outsourced areas is recognized. As Rebecca Birch pointed out in a recent presentation (1996), you need to make potential clients aware of your competence and reputation not only in the areas you are currently working on with them, but in all your areas of expertise.

In David Meyers' view (1996), an ideal project is a coherent, short-term intervention that can become integrated into the organization. For example, a project to develop performance improvement for supervisors should be designed as a self-sustaining system, so that developing new supervisors becomes a continuing responsibility for all managers in the client organization; and there is no need to have a project every few years to develop a new training course for supervisors.

This ideal outcome minimizes the risk posed by longer-term projects (i.e., because there is less time for changes to arise). But many projects cannot be completed in such a short timeframe. However, you can mitigate the risk of changing sponsors by organizing your project work so that the outcomes of individual project phases can be adapted immediately into the client organization's ongoing policies and practices. Report usable results as quickly as possible and encourage the customer to implement them immediately, without waiting for the entire project to be completed. For example, one of Mary's project teams is developing a training system that includes, among other elements, a series of job performance aids (JPA) to guide employee performance of critical tasks. As each JPA is reviewed, it is pilot tested and introduced immediately into the work setting. In this way, the customer has ongoing, tangible proof of the value of the project, and supervisors and employees have developed a level of confidence that the project will help them. This confidence level carries over into an acceptance of the more complex elements of the new training system.

Risk from Unclear Project Authority

Sometimes, you may be given the title of project manager but not the authority to manage the project. You may find that other people are making decisions about deadlines, staffing, and other aspects of the project without consulting you. These situations can place you at considerable risk because you will be responsible for outcomes based on decisions you did not make. You need to challenge the situation and make it clear that if you are not in control of the project, you cannot be responsible for the project outcomes. Clarify your role with your management as soon as this problem surfaces. Go over your project plan and identify all your resource needs and your cost-effective approach to meeting them. If your plan is not acceptable, it should be revised by your management, not surreptitiously by others. Ensure that you, and only you, will have sign-off authority to obtain and commit resources for the project, and send an e-mail message to all the stakeholders to this effect. As we said in chapter 3, you need to establish turf and responsibilities at the start of the project. You and your staff have a right to know who is in charge.

For example, you, the project manager, may have the best and most economical plan for procuring materials needed for a project, but if you don't lobby the appropriate people to implement it, you run the risk of having to spend your scarce project funds on a more expensive plan that was the old method of choice. This is not only not acceptable, but it may lead to your continuing a costly strategy that resulted in the decision to outsource in the first place! You can't be accountable for the project if others can reprogram your funds. You need to clearly explain your budget decisions and provide justification for them in terms of current business needs. Explain to the project sponsor, who is committing the funds, and to project advocates why your approach is best suited to meeting their previously stated objectives for the project. If you do not defend your project funding, you risk not only your own role as a project manager, but your project team's morale as they observe that resources they were depending on to accomplish tasks are being used inappropriately.

Risk and Reviewers

The process for reviewing the products or services your project generates can be very risky, especially if your continued funding depends on the delivery of acceptable products. Often work cannot continue on a subsequent task without approval of the preceding work. The best way to control this risk is by establishing clear and measurable review criteria that are known and agreed to by the stakeholders. For example, in designing customized information systems, subject matter experts often criticize the system interface and screen design as well as the actual content of the system. Screen design and interface design reviews, however, should be the bailiwick of end users. Feedback on new systems from subject matter experts and end users should be accepted freely during the review process, but you need to make clear whose feedback will carry the most weight in making final changes.

Criteria that spell out end users' requirements (e.g., can understand screen instructions, can complete necessary actions) and subject matter requirements (e.g., includes all necessary information, is legally correct) help reviewers focus on their own areas and help you distinguish between necessary and unnecessary revisions. Acceptance criteria should be tied to the decisions that must be made, so that an approval really does mean the project can proceed. Further, if there is a potential for disagreement on the decisions, make sure that the ultimate reviewer, or the person who has the final say, has been designated.

Before you submit project products for client review, you should, of course, have had them reviewed internally by objective reviewers. The first review should never be done by the client. Nothing blows your credibility more than a few typos or format errors that you should have caught before you gave the product to the customer. The same is true of even a rough prototype of a product. Make sure the agreed-to items are correct and complete and that the items you are testing are as clean as possible. This allows the customer to review the prototype without getting distracted by errors that are not related to the functionality you are trying to evaluate.

Often the selection of reviewers has political aspects. Stakeholders who lack the expertise to be good reviewers may be selected because they have influence over funding decisions or are interested in the project. You and the client must agree to who will review products and what qualifications they should have. Then, even if some of the reviewers are selected by your client's organization for political purposes (e.g., to secure their involvement and support), you can ensure that other reviewers will be selected based on the review qualification standards. Decide with your client what specific academic credentials and experience the reviewers who can recommend major changes should have. The opinion of a reviewer who does not have the necessary combination of education and experience is of little value in improving the product.

Reviewers need not only expertise to evaluate the work, but also willingness to commit the necessary time. Make your client aware that reviews must happen as scheduled and that when reviews are delayed, project work cannot continue. The risk here is that if the project is delayed you may lose project staff to other "revenue-producing" work and have difficulty getting them back later when project work begins again. Regardless of whether your project is one of several in an organization, or you are an independent entrepreneur and your project is staffed by consultants, only income-generating work can justify the commitment of staff. Make sure the organizations providing reviewers understand the importance and impact that this time commitment is.

You will need more than one type of reviewer, to ensure that all important stakeholder perspectives are represented. In the case of technical training materials, for instance, reviewers should include an expert who is highly knowledgeable about the technical content, another one who can judge the materials for educational values, and another who can judge whether the material is presented effectively in the type of format used. You and your customer will have to decide who will provide this review and whether it is up to the project team to find the reviewers or whether the customer will provide them. Most projects require both.

The people selected as reviewers are usually busy people. They are more likely to complete the review in a timely manner, and give you useful information, if you provide some guidance on how to complete the review. Mary Sand of the FAA recommends providing reviewers with five or six critical questions, such as: Is this content accurate? Does it cover the topic adequately? Have they adequately covered the background that supports this point? Do they give enough information about future use? Such questions speed up the reviews and provide useful feedback for revisions.

Risk and Quality

You should have a plan to ensure quality throughout the project. Anderson Consulting collects data on progress through client quality management assessments (CQMA). They survey both the project team and the client team to collect data on how well the work is being done, how the project is being managed, and how people are working together. These surveys and other project tracking documents are standardized across the company, which simplifies the project audits that are done periodically by CQMA reviewers not associated with the project. These reviewers know what documents they will be looking at and what data to look for. CQMA auditors take their responsibility very seriously because they are held accountable if a project they audited fails, and their audit did not identify the problems. When the audit is complete, the project manager discusses the findings and their implications with the client. For example, the audit findings may show that the budget estimates were too low, and that more money will be needed to complete the work unless the contract scope is scaled back.

If your project is small, you will not have as comprehensive a system as this, but you should still develop a quality assurance method suited to your own deliverables. Standardizing job processes at the beginning of the project will help ensure that people don't spend time reinventing the wheel in the form of developing different approaches to common tasks. If you standardize where possible at the beginning of the project, you will be better able to ensure that quality will be built in and reinforced throughout the life of the project, and your quality problems at the project conclusion will be minimized.

Because uncertainty presents serious risks to projects, organizations have done extensive research to identify the most likely risk factors and try to mitigate them. Bob Hunter of Anderson Consulting points out that his firm has 30,000 people and 900 partners, and any of them will be putting the firm at risk if a project is scoped or managed wrong. Answers to the question, What is the risk, and how do we manage it? are critical. Anderson Consulting has developed extensive training and many procedures to help people recognize and mitigate risk to the extent possible. In their organization, risk management is considered part of quality management. They reason that they can't provide quality if they don't deal with risk.

In recent years, Anderson's level of risk has increased, because the areas they work in have changed and they are dealing with new challenges. They are working in areas in which outcomes are unpredictable and trying to accomplish objectives that are different for each project and thus present unique challenges. For example, in projects that involve facilitating mergers and acquisitions, transforming industries, and creating start-ups, a certain level of chaos is expected; they try to manage the risk by continually collecting data on what happens. In this way, they build an experience base that over time increases their ability to better manage at least some parts of similar future projects. They also have customized existing software packages to manage some project tasks and fine-tuned their cost-estimating process so that they can more accurately predict the costs of specific pieces of the process.

Still, there are some projects where there is no experience on which to base cost estimates. You may start a project that requires skill and experience that are not available in the resources at your disposal. You can only make guesses, based on the requirements, as to what it will take to train people to the competency level that is needed or estimate how much it might cost to contract for people with the necessary skills. Risk is present in either case, because by the time you get the people trained or hired, you may or may not still need the skills. Again, you need to balance the short-term and long-term time, cost, and quality requirements as best you can, explaining your rationale clearly. These assumptions, that should be documented and remain visible to all the stakeholders, should be revisited regularly throughout the project to make sure they are still true. If not, you should recommend changes to the project plan that better meet the current requirements.

Technology Risks

Technology change is continual, representing a substantial risk to any project, especially in long-term projects and in projects that involve rapidly changing technology. Bob Woods, associate administrator for the General Services Administration (GSA) FTS 2000 project, which is developing the foundation for the new U.S. government telecommunications structure, recommends continually assessing the risk in planning for the development or use of technology as it evolves, converges, and changes in cost and capability.

His model looks at four levels of technology evolution. Depending on the timeframe of a project, technology that is not available at the project start may become available later and can require changes to your project. He illustrates these levels using concentric circles, as shown in Figure 7-1.

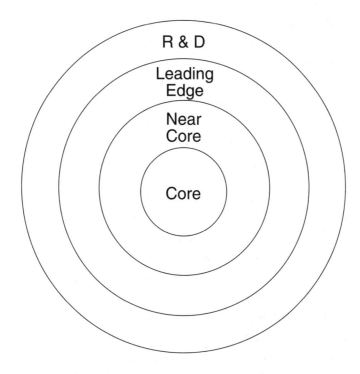

Figure 7-1. Risk Assessment Model

- Core technologies are in the center circle. They are the technologies we have now; for example: office software packages, PCs, workstations, faxes, scanners, imaging, workflow software, cellular phones.
- Near-core technologies are those that are likely to be available within six months; for example (as of this writing): Intranet systems now in use in some large corporations and digital versatile disk formats that can store 14 times as much information as today's CDs.

- Leading edge technologies are what is on the drawing board and may be ready for beta test within a year; for example: CAD/CAM software connected with data networks that program specifications directly into machines on production lines and smart phones that screen calls, check your e-mail, and do your banking.
- R & D technologies are still in the labs but have been written about and have the potential to result in products that will be of keen interest to your project; for example: webs of networked computers that receive orders and transmit them directly to mobile robots that broadcast what they need to the machine tools that determine how and when to do the work, with minimal human intervention and blue-laser CDs that will store all nine Beethoven symphonies.

Woods says a project manager must constantly monitor the progress of technologies as they move toward the core from the outer circles. For example, the FAA Advanced Automation System—a project to upgrade the air traffic control system—began before the advent of the personal computer. The project design was predicated on mainframe, vacuum tube technology. If it had been designed with the progress of technology in mind, it would have been possible to modify it to encompass advances in computer hardware and software, multimedia presentations, CD-ROM, interactive touch-screen terminals, and global positioning satellites. Our spiral model would have required pauses along the way to reassess the current situation and modify the design specifications to integrate these new technologies; indeed, the current AAS plan does include this type of flexibility.

New Technology

Introduce new technology whenever it is appropriate, but be sure it is really suited to the task. We are talking both about technology used as part of the solution or final product of the project, and the technology you use to assist in the project production process. Examples of the latter kind of technology include new CASE (computer-assisted engineering) tools, decision support tools, CBT or multimedia authoring tools, graphics design or production tools, or even project management or cost control tools. There are many risks to introducing a new technology to a project team to help you produce the product. Any new technology will involve a learning curve, and you should be certain that the benefits are great enough to warrant the cost of purchase and the even higher cost of time needed for team members to reach proficiency in its use.

One recent example of this was in the choice of a multimedia authoring tool to use for the development of training in a telecommunications company. When prototype lessons were being authored, the project team learned that the selected authoring tool could not simulate some of the functionality of the actual or real billing and customer contact system screens, the primary focus of the training. Too much was invested in the authoring system by that time, so the designers had to develop awkward explanations to the trainees about why the training lesson system screens looked different than the real system screems, a less-than-optimal solution to the problem. You can bet that this customer is going to look more carefully into any technology recommendation made by their project teams in the future.

Most of the project management software we have tried presents a real danger to its users. The software, with its power to change and update numbers and dates, seems to hypnotize project managers and their customers into thinking that the work of estimating and readjusting plans can be done just as easily. (If only. . . .) Don't let project management software based on linear project management models control your project. Project managers we talked with felt that project management software had very limited usefulness, because it could not accommodate the level of unpredictable real-time changes in schedules and staffing. However, they did find it useful for projects that entail extensive tracking of resources, for example, multimedia or construction projects. Those who are most enthusiastic about it have developed macros that tailor the software to their needs. But be careful that you don't end up managing the schedule, rather than the project. We have included some project management software programs and resources for macros in our reference list.

Contingency Budgeting

Because risk is endemic in all projects, it is critical to build into the budget some allowance for what Karen Taylor of ELF calls nightmares—situations that are totally unforeseen and different on every project. Sometimes, project budgets should include contingency items to deal with these types of cost. In the case of a project that has unique characteristics for which there is no experience base, Anderson Consulting will sometimes include in its project budget a contingency line item, valued at 10 to 20 percent of the total project. This item is intended to cover costs incurred that could not have been anticipated, for example, a new computer system that goes down unexpectedly, through no fault of either the project or the client. If the contingency budget is not needed, it is not billed against. A contingency should not be confused with a change in scope, which can be defined and specifically budgeted for.

Conclusion Stage Risks

The major risk at the project conclusion stage is in failing to document lessons learned, because if you don't do this, you are prone to repeat the same errors in your next project. If you are following the model we outlined in chapter 3, you can set aside time at the end of each stage and implementation spiral to meet with your project team to document what you learned and discuss how you can apply it in the remaining project stages and spirals.

Before project team members who have completed their tasks move on to other projects, you should meet with them and discuss their experiences. Thank them for their contribution, tell them how you plan to recognize their work, and ask them what they think went well and what improvements they think are needed. Don't wait until the end of the project—the entire team may have moved on to other things, and you yourself will be looking forward to another project.

Know When to Fold

Project managers, like poker players, need to know when to fold, or conclude a project, a sometimes difficult proposition. People tend to become very involved and have a hard time letting go, especially if they have been working with a compatible team. A complex project can take up a major part of the team members' lives, sometimes for a year or more. It seems that, just when it is going well or that it is getting under control, it's time to end the project.

Clients also become accustomed to the project manager and the team and forget that they are only temporary resources. They may continue to ask for briefings or multiple extra copies of products long after the project budget is depleted. As the project manager, you have to decide whether the best course is to present them with a proposal for additional work, or to charge the additional work to ongoing marketing to the organization. The risk is in committing time and resources out of habit, without requiring the client to acknowledge that these are new and unfunded requirements. It is best, for everyone's sake, to schedule a final project briefing for all stakeholders. In this meeting, celebrate the achievements of the project goals, reminisce about shared experiences, display the project products, and thank everyone who contributed to the project success.

Abandoned Projects

Sometimes a project that is considered urgent at its start, after an initial period of client commitment is suddenly abandoned as unneeded and valueless. Such disastrous situations should not happen, of course, if the project had been correctly scoped. But as we have said before, circumstances change, and nothing is certain. However, experienced project managers have developed strategies to salvage something from such projects.

One strategy, if you think the project is worthwhile and the client really needs it, is to carefully document the project and file it in a "parking lot" to be driven out again at a later date, when the client is again aware of the problem the project was designed to address.

Another strategy is to explore the possibility of scaling down the project, so that some important parts survive. Lori and Mary's students are tired of being reminded to "rescope," but that's often the appropriate strategy. Scaling down the project can ensure that some important parts of the project survive.

For example, a multiyear project to develop a pay-for-skills compensation plan was terminated when it was discovered that another region had developed a plan, had it approved by the company and the union, and was putting it in place. The project manager was told that the other region's compensation plan would be adapted to the client's department, so that the project to develop a new plan was no longer needed. The project manager suggested, instead, that members of the project team show the client how to adapt the existing plan to the different work processes, tasks, and employee skill sets in the local region, so that the plan for the new work force would meet legal and union scrutiny.

Summary

For every risk we have listed, there is at least one (or many) we haven't mentioned. Which areas of uncertainty and risk that will affect your project depend upon the particular environment, people, and situation involved and interacting at the time. Our warning and advice: Don't underestimate the risk in your actions. Newton wasn't wrong when he stated that for every action there is an equal and opposite reaction. This rule, one of the three laws of physics he discovered, remains true in organizations and projects. Quantum physics reminds us to look beyond at the unpredictable effect that an initial action has on other interactions that spin off from those initial actions and reactions.

Risk assessment allows you to consider the effects of your interactions before you have changed the reality into one that you didn't intend. You obviously can't predict all of the risks for all of your actions, and who would want to? You would paralyze yourself just thinking about them. Maybe the better lesson, and better vision of risk management, is the one our parents used to remind us of: Look before you leap. Make sure there is a surface on which you can land safely on the other side.

Chapter 8

Putting It All Together: Taking the Quantum Leap

Is what we've been talking about new? Is our model for project management that much different from the traditional model? Yes—and no. We have deliberately set out to not redesign the world, or at least, the project management part of it. What we hope we have provided is a new way to apply aspects of other models in an iterative, "spiral" approach to succeed as project conditions inevitably change. We have tried to share with you what many of us have discovered, sometimes the hard way, that successful project management results from a positive, holistic, flexible state of mind and a practical, systematic approach that deals with change, risk, and uncertainty as an ongoing responsibility.

Project Management Critical Success Factors

In our interviews, focus groups, and research, we have received many definitions of what "success" is in project management. The one we most commonly heard is the following:

Project management is successful when the desired project results are achieved or produced on time and within budget.

Given that definition, our approach to project management will never be widely accepted. We however, do have a replacement definition to offer:

Project management is successful when the desired project results are achieved or produced in a way that is satisfactory to all the project stakeholders.

We suggest that our definition is more holistic and systemic; takes into account the multiple ways of evaluating project success, rather than pinning success to the measures of dollars and time. There were many reasons projects were reported to be "failures," and few of them had anything to do with time or money.

What we would encourage you to do is set up your project for success by establishing with your stakeholders the critical success factors for your project and its management. These should include factors to evaluate both the **project process**, or how well the work of the project went and was managed, and the **project results**, or how the project or product you produced and implemented worked according to what was expected or desired. We cannot give you any specific recommendations on the critical success factors for project results; these would have to be directly related to your project goals and objectives and the actual product and product user you are targeting. On project process, however, we do have a few suggestions. The critical success factors listed in Table 8-1 have been mentioned throughout the previous chapters but are listed here as a summary.

Lessons Learned

Table 8-1. Project Management Critical Success Factors

Project Stages	Critical Success Factors
Opportunity	• Client and project manager have the same project approach philosophy. • Data (or money and time to collect data) exist to correctly scope and resource project. • Correct problem is identified and analyzed. • All assumptions of client and project manager identified and agreed upon. • Long-term, high-level support is assured.
Commitment	• Client expectations realistic—This is what we can do with this budget and in this timeframe. • Necessary information available to write a realistic proposal. • Cost of developing proposal appropriate to anticipated return on investment. • Contingency budget is agreed to and in place. • Project plan flexible enough to incorporate changes as needed. • All stakeholders' roles and responsibilities identified and agreed to. • Project team appropriate for project tasks. • Project team working approach and environment established.
Implementation	• Early prototype cycles provides adequate feedback for revision/rescoping for next implementation spiral. • Value-added options identified and addressed. • Scope changes accompanied by additional resources. • Appropriate reviewers and testers selected. • Client ensures timely reviews. • Quality control system in place and followed.
Conclusion	• Client satisfied with outcomes and process—probably will want to work with you again. • Project completed by negotiated due date and within revised budget. • Project team pleased with outcomes and process—probably will want to work with you again. • Project results in return on investment as anticipated.

What have we learned from our experiences and the experiences of others in project management? We learned that our old models for project management do not and cannot manage all aspects of the dynamic change process involved in managing a project. We've learned that risk and uncertainty are always present and that dealing with them head on leads to more successful project outcomes than ignoring them. We've also learned that we need to focus much more on the process of change rather than on the objects (for example, the technology) of change. Specific lessons we have learned are listed in the following. Again, these lessons have been mentioned previously but are presented here as a summary.

- Don't take on a project unless you can be a partner with the client. You should never just be a vendor delivering work for pay.
- Select clients carefully. If you want a collaborative relationship, don't try to work with a client with a win/lose attitude.
- Be sure you know who all the "real" clients are.
- Clarify assumptions about resources, reviewers, contingencies, and so on up front.
- Get to know the end users early and involve them in prototyping.
- Be a partner to your client and your suppliers and vendors.
- Add value beyond what is required.
- Pay attention to the training and development issues—your team's and your client's.
- Have a formal ending to the project—don't let it continue after resources are depleted.

Strategies for Coping with Uncertainty

We believe our recommended project management model integrates a more realistic view of projects and their expected results by incorporating a quantum physics view of reality with our sociotechnical engineering view of organizational project work. We have developed and do practice certain strategies for coping with this new picture of reality. These strategies are based both on our experience in complex technology change projects and on a quantum physics view. We recommend them to you for your next project manager stint.

- Embrace and live with uncertainty.
- Be proactive; anticipate uncertainty.
- Develop and use a risk assessment model.
- Focus on the process of change, not the tools.

Embrace and Live with Uncertainty

- Accept disorder, complexity, instability, nonlinearity, non-predictability. Instead of fighting them, build in activities and methods to deal with the unpredictable results and related confusion as part of your project plan.
- Never assume you can determine all the parts of the whole picture at the start of the project.
- Do not oversimplify: Assess risk constantly.

Be Proactive: Anticipate Uncertainty

- Develop a flexible project plan that allows you to regroup when the unpredictable happens. Sell your plan and approach to your sponsors and stakeholders. Make sure they understand the unreality of trying to determine all the details up front.
- Identify and communicate with all stakeholders and solicit their ideas.
- Build in ways to communicate easily with new stakeholders as they emerge.
- Develop prototypes and get rapid feedback on what might need to change.
- Build reassessment and modification points into your plan.

Develop and Use a Risk Assessment Model

In assessing the risk related to technology change, we like using the model developed by Bob Wood, of GSA (as we showed you in Figure 7-1). Using that model, you can assess the proposed technology, then incorporate into your plan any of the technologies that would be appropriate for your effort as they become available. This risk assessment model can also be adapted to assess risks in other areas, such as organizational environment, organizational structures, organizational culture, and employee performance requirements.

For example, a worker can assess the risk he or she faces in retaining employability in the job market. Core job skills in a traditional organization are outlined in an employee's job description. This document typically outlines what the employee is expected to do and under what supervision and documents the education and work experience that the job incumbent should have. The worker can probably meet these current requirements, at least minimally.

Near the core will be additional requirements; for example, that workers know what business the organization is in and how their unit and their own specific tasks contribute to accomplishing the business objectives. To meet these near-core requirements, workers would have to be cross-trained so that they are able to do other jobs in their unit. Another near-core requirement might be that workers will be expected to have excellent interpersonal skills to work productively in self-directed worker teams that organize and carry out their work autonomously.

At the leading edge, and eventually expected to be incorporated into all organizations, job requirements will encompass a wide range of constantly changing skills and a need for employees to continuously expand their skills repertoire. There will be extensive on-line help to guide correct performance, and many paper-based tasks will be eliminated, as electronic commerce and other technologies are introduced.

At the R & D stage, job requirements of the future will be formulated to take advantage of new technology, research into brain functions, and ergonomics. Work teams will be able to work together on-line, from any location, and productivity measures will improve.

A young worker, using a risk assessment model in planning a career can be certain that competence in advanced technologies, flexibility and a commitment to lifelong learning, and the skill to work productively with others will be keys to employability in the future.

Regardless of the risk assessment model you use, assess risk often, incorporating new findings into your project as they emerge.

Focus on the Process of Change, Not the Tools of Change

Donella Meadows, in an article "Whole Earth Models and Systems" (Meadows, 1982, 23), quotes an ancient Sufi teaching that directs us toward this strategy. "You think because you understand *one* you must understand *two*, because one and one make two. But you must also understand *and*."

Quantum physics tells us that we cannot predict what will be created by the interactions of particles and waves, but it does provide us with the framework for understanding how that interaction and the situation surrounding that interaction influence the next creation and the next interaction. It teaches us that the *and* is where we must focus our attention, provide guidance and assistance, and look for answers. For it is here that real change takes place.

Reference List

Abrams, Joe and George Smith. "Business Process Re-engineering." *Imaging World* (June 1, 1996): 34-36.

Andrews, Dorine and Susan Stalick. *Business Reengineering*. Englewood Cliffs, NJ: Yourdon Press, 1994.

Atkinson, Rick. "Platoons of Plans Shaped Army's Shove into Bosnia." *Washington Post* (December 29, 1995): A1, A27.

Baker, Bruce N.; David C. Murphy; and Dalmar Fisher. *Determinants of Project Success,* #N-74-30392. Springfield, VA: NTIS, September 1974.

Banathy, Bela H. "Creating Our Future in an Age of Transformation." *Performance Improvement Quarterly* 7, 3 (1994): 87-102.

Bancroft, Nancy. *New Partnerships for Managing Technological Change*. New York: John Wiley & Sons, Inc., 1992.

Beckhard, Richard and Reuben Harris. *Organizational Transitions: Managing Complex Change*. Reading, MA: Addison-Wesley, 1977.

Bell, Alan. "Next Generation Compact Discs." *Scientific American* (July 1996): 42.

Birch, Rebecca. "Publicizing All Your Capabilities." Presentation at ISPI Potomac Chapter meeting (April 1996).

Birk, Thomas A. and John E. Burk. "The Impact of Communication on Organizational Change: Interpreting Corporate Cultures." Presentation at ISPI Annual Conference (April 1996).

Block-Petrella-Weisbord. *Improving Whole Systems: A Guidebook*. Plainfield, NJ: Block-Petrella-Weisbord, Inc., 1992.

Boehm, B.W. "A Spiral Model of Software Development and Enhancement." *IEEE Computer* 21, 5 (1988): 61-72.

Bridges, William. "The End of the Job." *Fortune* (September 19, 1994): 62-74.

Burns, Robert. "To a Mouse." *The Literature of England*. Chicago: Scott Foresman & Co., 1941, 104.

Caldwell, B. "Missteps, Miscues, Reengineering Slipups." *Information Week* (June 20, 1994): 50-60.

Carey, John and Heidi Dawley. "Science's New Nano Frontier." *Business Week* (July 1, 1996): 101-102.

Carr, Clay. *Choice, Chance and Organizational Change*. New York: AMACOM, 1996.

Carroll, Lewis. *Alice's Adventures in Wonderland*. New York: Washington Square Press, 1960.

Carter, Delores. "Networking." Presentation at Delta Kappa Gamma State Convention, Bethesda, Maryland (May 5, 1996).

Cebula, Rick. Hughes STX. Interview with Mary DeWeaver, March 12, 1996.

Conner, Daryl R. *Managing at the Speed of Change.* New York: Villard Books, 1995.

Cotello, Nick. "Practicing Safe Schedules." *Multimedia Producer* (May 1996): 71.

Cowie, Rosalind. Government Accounting Office. Interview, February 23, 1996.

Curley, Terence and Marilyn A. Hawkins. "Eating the Elephant in One Bite." Presentation at the Organizational Systems Designers Conference, Washington, DC, 1996.

deHoog, Robert; Ton de Jong; and Frits de Vries. "Constraint Driven Software Design: An Escape from the Waterfall Model." *Performance Improvement Quarterly* 7, 3 (1994): 48-63.

DeWeaver, Mary and Amy Titus, facilitators. Focus Group on Project Management at ISPI Potomac Chapter Workshop Extravaganza (May 21, 1996).

Dobrovolny, Jackie; Lori Gillespie; and Tim Spannaus. "Managing the Virtual Project." Presentation at the ISPI Conference, Dallas, Texas (April 1996).

Dormant, Diane. "Planning Change: Past, Present, Future." In S. Thiagarajan and P. McGillis, eds., *The Guidebook for Performance Improvement.* San Francisco: Pfeiffer, 1997.

Duck, Jeanie D. "Managing Change: The Art of Balancing." *Harvard Business Review* (November-December, 1993): 109-118.

Esque, Timm. "Accomplishment-Based Project Planning— Intel." Presentation at ISPI Conference, Dallas, Texas (April 1996).

Esque, Timm. "Eventful Interventions." *Performance Improvement* (October 1996): 30-32.

Farrell, Christopher; Michael Mandel; and Joseph Weber. "The Productivity Bonanza." *Business Week* (October 9, 1995): 146.

Farrell, Kathy and Craig Broude. *Winning the Change Game.* Wellesley, MA: QED Information Sciences, Inc., 1987.

Fashay, Wellesley R. TRO Learning, Inc. Interview with Lori Gillespie, January 20, 1996.

Fossum, Lynn. *Understanding Organizational Change: Converting Theory to Practice.* Los Altos, CA: Crisp Publications, Inc., 1989.

Gillespie, L. and Budd M. Sneller. "Goedkoper en Effectiever Opleiden" [Getting Them to the Job Faster, Cheaper and More Effectively]. *Praktisch Personeelsbelied/Capita Selecta* - afl. 8. Deventer, The Netherlands: Uitgeverij Kluwer bv. (1984).

Gingrande, Arthur. "Tips on Managing an Imaging Project." *Imaging World* (May 23, 1994): 4.

Harrington, Walt. "How Can This Be Happening? When the Ax Fell at USGS." *Washington Post Magazine* (May 19, 1996): 15-21, 29-30.

Hillelsohn, Michael. "Been There, Done That: Some Lessons Learned on Software Development Contracts." *Crosstalk* (May 1996): 23-28.

Hunter, Robert. Interview, April 11, 1996.

Kamaradt, Beth. Eli Lilly and Company. Interview, May 29, 1996.

Kirk, Margaret. "When Surviving Just Isn't Enough." *New York Times* (Sunday, June 25, 1995): 11.

Koroscil, Ron and Jack D'Urso. "Pitney Bowes Manufacturing and Facility Support." Presentation at ISPI Potomac Chapter Workshop Extravaganza (May 21, 1996).

Kozel, Kathy. "The Interactive Killing Fields." *Multimedia Producer* (May 1996): 69-71, 82-86, 100-102.

Krutch, Joseph Wood. *The Twelve Seasons.* Salem, NH: Index Reprint Series, 1949. (Out of print.)

Mandel, Michael J. "Business Rolls the Dice." *Business Week* (October 17, 1994): 89-90.

Mathews, Rick; Maureen Taylor; Mario Gosalves; and Malinda Cirimele. "Teaming Up in Cyberspace: A Virtual Adventure in Learning." *Performance & Instruction* 35, 5 (May-June 1996): 16-20.

Meadows, D. "Whole Earth Models and Systems." *Co-Evolution Quarterly* (Summer 1982): 98-108.

Meyers, David. Human Technology, Inc. Interview with Mary DeWeaver, February 12, 1996.

Mintz, John. "Panel Issues Findings on Air Traffic Control Outages." *Washington Post* (January 20, 1996), D-1.

Moore, James. *The Death of Competition.* New York: Harper Business Books, 1996, Chapter 4.

Morris, Michele. "Career Control: Happy Home, Healthy Business." *Executive Female* (November-December 1991): 29.

Nelson, Harold G. "The Necessity of Being 'Un-Disciplined' and 'Out of Control': Design Action and Systems Thinking." *Performance Improvement Quarterly* 7, 3 (1994): 22-29.

Petroski, Henry. *To Engineer Is Human: The Role of Failure in Successful Design.* New York: Vintage Books, 1992.

Ricklefs, Roger. "Restless Youth." *Wall Street Journal: Report on Small Business* (May 23, 1996): R18.

Rittel, Horst. "On the Planning Crisis: Systems Analysis of the 'First and Second Generations'." *Bedrifts Okonomen* 8 (1972): 390-396.

Sand, Mary. Federal Aviation Administration. Interview with Mary DeWeaver, March 19, 1996.

Schellhardt, Timothy D. "David in Goliath." *Wall Street Journal: Report on Small Business* (May 23, 1996): R14.

Senge, Peter. *The Fifth Discipline.* New York: Doubleday, 1990.

Shellenbarger, Sue. "Enter the New Hero: The Boss Who Knows You Have a Life." *Wall Street Journal* (May 8, 1996): B1.

Sink, Darryl. "Designing in a High-Change Environment." Presentation at the ISPI Conference, Dallas, Texas (April 1996).

Smith, Lee. "New Ideas from the Army." *Fortune* (September 19, 1994): 212

Software Engineering Institute. *Software Acquisition Capability Maturity Model* SM *(SA-CMM*SM*)*, No. SA-CMM 96-03. Pittsburgh, PA: Carnegie Mellon University, April 1996.

Spannaus, Tim. Emdicium, Inc. Interviews with Lori Gillespie, January-April, 1996.

Spolar, Christine. "Balkan River Swamps Army's Bridge Plans." *Washington Post* (December 29, 1995): A1, A27.

Stalcup, Betsy. "How Can This Be Happening? When the Ax Fell at USGS." *Washington Post Magazine* (May 19, 1996): 6.

Stalick, Susan. Combating Counterterrorist Tactics in Business Reengineering Projects. Presentation at ISPI Conference, Dallas, Texas (April 1996).

Stine, G. Harry. "The Rooster Crows at White Sands." *Analog Science Fiction and Fact* (May 1994): 64-73.

Stine, G. Harry. "Why Build Experimental Vehicles?" *Analog Science Fiction and Fact* (June 1995): 4-14.

Taylor, Karen. Electronic Learning Facilitators, Inc. Interview with Mary DeWeaver and Lori Gillespie, January 30, 1996.

Titus, Amy. Titus Austin, Inc. Interview with Mary DeWeaver, February 19, 1996.

Trenkle, T. Interview with Mary DeWeaver. Washington, DC, GSA Headquarters, July 22, 1994.

Turner, John. Federal Aviation Administration. Interview with Mary DeWeaver, May 27, 1994.

U.S. General Accounting Office. *The New Job Process: Instructor Manual, Release 2.* Washington, DC: GAO Training Institute (January 22, 1996).

U.S. General Accounting Office. *Air Traffic Control: Observations on Proposed Corporation,* GAO/T-RCED-94-210 Washington, DC: GAO (1994).

U.S. General Services Administration. *Information Technology Pilot Projects: Keys to Success.* Washington, DC: GSA (November 1995).

Valone, Robert M. "The Advanced Automation System." Lecture at Catholic University, Washington, DC, July 1, 1994.

Vaughan, Diane. "Risky Business. How NASA Blew Up the Challenger." *Boston College Magazine* (Spring 1996): 24-36.

Weiner, Jonathan. *The Beak of the Finch: A Story of Evolution in Our Time.* New York: Knopf, 1994.

Weintraub, R.M. "FAA Grounds Two Key Parts of Big Computer Project." *Washington Post* (June 4, 1994): B4.

Wheatley, Margaret. *Leadership and the New Science.* San Francisco, CA: Berrett-Koehler, 1992.

Wiggenhorn, William. "Total Customer Satisfaction at Motorola, Inc." Presentation at NSPI Conference (1988.)

Wysocki, Jr., Bernard. "High-Tech Nomads Write New Programs for Future of Work." *Wall Street Journal* (August 19, 1996): A1, A6.

Zuboff, S. *In the Age of the Smart Machine.* New York: Basic Books, 1988.

Project Management Bibliography

Badiru, Adedeji and Simon Pulat. *Comprehensive Project Management: Integrating Optimization Models, Management Principles and Computers.* Upper Saddle River, NJ: Prentice Hall Professional Technical Reference, 1994.

Cleland, David I. *Project Management: Strategies, Design and Implementation.* New York: McGraw-Hill Book Company, 1994.

Frame, Davidson J. *Managing Projects in Organizations: How to Make the Best Use of Time, Techniques and People.* San Francisco: Jossey-Bass, 1995.

Frame, Davidson J. *The New Project Management: Tools for an Age of Rapid Change, Corporate Reengineering, and Other Business Realities.* San Francisco: Jossey-Bass, 1994.

Golas, Katherine C. "Estimating Time to Develop Interactive Courseware in the '90's." *Journal of Interactive Instructional Development* (Winter 1994).

Greer, Michael. *ID (Instructional Development) Project Management: Tools and Techniques for Instructional Designers and Developers,* 1992.

House, Ruth Sizemore. *The Human Side of Project Management*. Beverly, MA: Addison-Wesley, 1988.

Ince, Darrel; Helen Sharp; and Mark Woodman. *Introduction to Software Project Management and Quality Assurance*. New York: McGraw-Hill Book Company, 1993.

Kerzner, Harold. *Project Management: A Systems Approach to Planning, Scheduling and Controlling*. New York: Van Nostrand Reinhold, 1994.

Kharbanda, O.P. and Jeffrey K. Pinto. *What Made Gertie Gallop? Learning from Project Failures*. New York: Van Nostrand Reinhold, 1996.

Lewis, James P. *Fundamentals of Project Management*. New York: AMACOM, 1995.

Lewis, James P. *Project Planning, Scheduling and Control: A Hands-On Guide to Bringing Projects in On Time and On Budget*. Norcross, GA: Engineering and Management Press, 1995.

Marca, David and Clement McGowan. *SADT: Structured Analysis and Design Technique*. New York: McGraw-Hill Book Company, 1988.

Northrup, Pamela Taylor. "Concurrent Formative Evaluation: Guidelines and Implications for Multimedia Designers." *Educational Technology* (November-December 1995).

Shtub, Abraham; Jonathan Bard; and Shlomo Globerson. *Project Management: Engineering, Technology, and Implementation*. Upper Saddle River, NJ: Prentice Hall Engineering Science and Math, 1994.

Thomsett, Rob. *Third Wave Project Management: A Handbook for Managing the Complex Information Systems for the 1990's.* Englewood Cliffs, NJ: Prentice Hall, 1989.

Turtle, Quentin C. *Implementing Concurrent Project Management.* Upper Saddle River, NJ: Prentice Hall Professional Technical Reference, 1994.

Zemke, Ron and Thomas Kramlinger. *Figuring Things Out, A Trainer's Guide to Needs and Task Analysis.* New York: Addison-Wesley, 1982.

Index

resource definition in, 83–92

risk management, proposals, and
commitments in, 92–94,
180–184

setting timelines and output
specifications in, 78–80

tasks and activities, 64–66

who is involved in, 66–69, 128,
130

communication plan, for introducing changes, 171–173

communication strategies, in the
commitment stage, 71–72

communications, 161, 187

competition, 8

as a risk to projects, 16, 28–30

conclusion stage, 45–46

definition of, 106–107

documentation and transfer
technology in, 109–111

final approval in, 108–109

questions to resolve in,
107–108

risks in, 198–201

saying good-bye in, 111–112

conducting business through
projects, 2

conflict, dealing with, 155–156

contingency budgeting, 198

costs, 10, 194 (*see also* funding)

creativity, 80–82

cross-functional team, 70

customer demands, 22

customer relationships, 15

customer requirements, 8

customers

education of, 134–135

focus on during implementation
stage, 104

networking with, 117

and staffing, 128

as stakeholders, 58–61, 120–121

data

availability of, 26

gathering and analysis, 53, 70,
193–194

and the opportunity stage, 61

decision making, 81–82

delegating, 157–158

deliverable schedule, 25

deliverables, 79–80, 85, 88

design concept, 49

design matrix for stakeholder
communication, 55–57

division of work, 70–71

documentation, 80–82, 88

in the conclusion stage, 108–111

and CQMA, 192

of lessons learned, 198–199

reviewing, 158–159

downsizing, 8, 12

economy, 1, 8

role of newly independent entrepreneur in, 13

education, 18

of the customer, 134–135

end users, 58, 190

focus on during the implementation stage, 104

keeping in the loop, 130–131

networking with, 117

resistance of, 26–27

as stakeholders, 59–61, 120–121

environments

changing, 42

as sources of risks, 29–30

expectations, changing, 184–185

experienced project managers, 3, 16

expertise, lack of, 35–36

experts

knowledge of, 129–130

networking with, 117

as stakeholders, 59, 120

leadership responsibility, of the
project manager as politician,
127–128
linear approach to project
management, 21–22
long-term projects, and technology risks, 194–196

natural science, and change, 19
networking
definition of, 116
during the opportunity stage, 61
for incorporating change, 168
by the project manager,
116–118, 133
new technical professional, 3,
14–15
newly independent entrepreneur,
2, 12–13
Newtonian universe, 163–164

objectives
changing, 42
in the opportunity stage, 61
opportunity stage, 44–46, 84,
94–95, 183, 185
definition of, 48–51
organizational example of,
54–57
output of, 61–62
questions to be resolved in,
49–50, 54
reassessment during implementation stage, 104
risk assessment in, 53–54
risk management in, 175–180
tasks and activities, 51–52
who is involved in, 57–61, 130
organizational mission, 76
output specifications, setting,
78–80
overhead, 9

partnerships, creation by the
project manager, 122–130
people resources, 83–86
performance
improvement of, 156–157
self-assessment of, 149–150
physical resources, 77
physical science, as regards
uncertainty and change,
18–19
politics
and reviewers, 190–191
role of project manager in, 135
proactive approach
to change, 1
for anticipating uncertainty, 207
problem definition, 49–52
problem solving, 31–32, 156
problems with project management approaches, 10–11
product design and development,
76
in the implementation stage,
99–100
professional association meetings,
use of, 133
professional direction, 158–159
professional interests, project
manager as broker of,
151–152
project approaches, 98–103, 106,
112–113
project authority, unclear,
188–189
project completion, 9, 199–200
(*see also* conclusion stage)
project failures, 27–29, 35, 115,
117, 204
due to lack of value analysis and
buy in, 62
and quality, 137
project longevity, risk and, 186

review of, 190
use of, 79–80, 172
public relations, 77–78

quality
of products, 142
and risk, 192–194
standards, 156
of work, 10, 137
quality professionals, and project
management, 17–18
quantum physics
and reality, 39, 164, 201, 206–207
and technology, 19
quantum view, 78, 115, 209

rapid prototyping
methodology, 101–102
models, 98
reengineering projects, 161–163
relationships, effect on success, 45
rescoping of projects, 28–29
resources, 45, 83–88
return on investment, 10, 12
as a risk to projects, 16
review process and criteria,
73–74, 190–192
reviewers, and risk, 189–191
rewards, to team members,
145–146
risk assessment, 43, 47, 201
during the commitment stage,
74–75
during the implementation stage,
98–100, 102–103
during the opportunity stage,
53–54, 175–177
by the GAO, 93–94
model for, 195–196, 207–209
risk management, 73–74, 175
during commitment stage,
92–94, 180–184

during conclusion stage,
198–201
during implementation stage,
184–198
during the opportunity stage,
175–180
risks, 1, 3
and changing expectations,
184–185
and contingency budgeting, 198
delays as a source of, 135
and direction of a project, 45
as a given, 43
in the implementation stage, 97
minimizing, 70–71, 78, 81
mitigating, 90–91, 130
and new technology introduction, 196–198
in not concluding a project,
199–200
organizational and environmental, 62
and project longevity, 186
in projects versus traditional
work organizations, 7
and quality, 192–194
related to change in sponsor,
186–187
and reviewers, 189–191
sources of, 29–30, 87
of technology, 194–196
from unclear project authority,
188–189
working relationships as buffer
for, 155–156
roles and responsibilities
during the commitment stage, 67
tested by turf boundaries, 69

schedules, 80–82
scope creep, as a risk to projects,
16, 185

self-development
  for the project manager, 146–150
  of virtual teams, 153–154
self-managed team leader, 3,
    15–16
short-term results, deadlines for, 79
sociotechnical engineering model,
    161, 206
soft technology, 91–92
specification and planning, 47
spiral models, 45–48, 61, 196,
    203
  in conclusion stage, 108, 199
  in implementation stage, 64,
    98–100, 102–103, 105
sponsors
  and change adoption, 168
  networking with, 117
  as resources, 84–86
  risks related to change in,
    186–187
  as stakeholders, 58–61, 104,
    118–119
staff, 9
  influence on technology, 89
  just-in-time, 138–139
  lean and mean, 141–142
  productive use of, 10
  roles and responsibilities of, 67
  selection of, 128–129
  and time estimation risks, 181
  training and development of,
    150–152
stakeholder goals, as sources of
    risk, 29–30
stakeholders, 24–27
  and change, 164–173
  in the commitment stage, 66–69
  customers as, 58
  eroding support of, 37
  failure to involve, 36
  feedback from, 33

and final product approval, 109
GAO design matrix for commu-
    nication with, 55–57
identification and analysis of,
    58–61
and the implementation stage,
    103–104
influence on projects, 42
influence on technology, 89
informing, 95
networking with, 116–117
and the opportunity stage, 52–57
relating with, 118–122
and review criteria, 190–192
roles of, 69–70
standardizing, 193
steering committee, 60
subcontractors. *See* suppliers
suppliers
  networking with, 117
  as a partner, 132
  as stakeholders, 59–60, 121
support systems, 76–77
systems development, classic, 101

tame problems, 31–32
technology, 15
  activities, 76
  advances in, 1
  and a change project, 170–171,
    207
  development approaches for, 102
  improvements in, 22
  inappropriate, 36
  new, 196–198
  and quantum physics, 19
  as a resource, 86, 89–92
  as a risk to projects, 16, 27,
    29–30, 54, 194–196
  selection of, 90
  transfer of, 109–111
testing and review, 47